CELEBRATING IN A PLC AT WORK®

A LEADER'S GUIDE TO
Building Collective Efficacy and
High-Performing Collaborative Teams

David T. Chiprany and Phillip Page

Solution Tree | Press

Copyright © 2025 by Solution Tree Press

Materials appearing here are copyrighted. With one exception, all rights are reserved. Readers may reproduce only those pages marked "Reproducible." Otherwise, no part of this book may be reproduced or transmitted in any form or by any means (electronic, photocopying, recording, or otherwise) without prior written permission of the publisher.

555 North Morton Street
Bloomington, IN 47404
800.733.6786 (toll free) / 812.336.7700
FAX: 812.336.7790

email: info@SolutionTree.com
SolutionTree.com

Visit **go.SolutionTree.com/PLCbooks** to download the free reproducibles in this book.

Printed in the United States of America

Library of Congress Cataloging-in-Publication Data

Names: Chiprany, David T., author. | Page, Phillip, author.
Title: Celebrating in a PLC at work® : a leader's guide to building
   collective efficacy and high-performing collaborative teams / David T.
   Chiprany, Phillip Page.
Other titles: Celebrating in a professional learning community at work
Description: Bloomington, IN : Solution Tree Press, [2025] | Includes
   bibliographical references and index.
Identifiers: LCCN 2024038750 (print) | LCCN 2024038751 (ebook) | ISBN
   9781958590232 (paperback) | ISBN 9781958590249 (ebook)
Subjects: LCSH: Professional learning communities. | Team learning approach
   in education. | Teaching teams. | Educational leadership.
Classification: LCC LB1731 .C446 2025 (print) | LCC LB1731 (ebook) | DDC
   371.14/8--dc23/eng/20240821
LC record available at https://lccn.loc.gov/2024038750
LC ebook record available at https://lccn.loc.gov/2024038751

Solution Tree
Jeffrey C. Jones, CEO
Edmund M. Ackerman, President

Solution Tree Press
President and Publisher: Douglas M. Rife
Associate Publishers: Todd Brakke and Kendra Slayton
Editorial Director: Laurel Hecker
Art Director: Rian Anderson
Copy Chief: Jessi Finn
Senior Production Editor: Suzanne Kraszewski
Text and Cover Designer: Julie Csizmadia
Acquisitions Editors: Carol Collins and Hilary Goff
Content Development Specialist: Amy Rubenstein
Associate Editors: Sarah Ludwig and Elijah Oates
Editorial Assistant: Anne Marie Watkins

I dedicate this book to my wife, Diane. Her encouragement throughout my professional journey has been unconditional and inspiring. You are my best friend.

—David T. Chiprany

I dedicate this book to my wife, Colleen. She has always been my inspiration and motivation in all areas of life. I love you!

—Phillip Page

Acknowledgments

In 2018, we had the opportunity to lead the Bartow County School System in Georgia as superintendent and deputy superintendent. This book is possible because of a school system and community coming together to create a culture shift focused on celebrating staff and students throughout the process of building a systemwide Professional Learning Community at Work® (PLC at Work). We would like to express our sincere gratitude to Jeffery Jones and Mike Mattos for their guidance in our three-year implementation timeline. This plan was our guide for progress monitoring, supporting, and celebrating the incredible culture shift that transformed our schools, school system, and community. We would also like to thank Jasmine Kullar, who introduced us to the PLC process, and to Rich Smith, who guided us through our RTI work and encouraged us as we navigated the barriers to learning for all students.

Furthermore, we are thankful for the amazing teachers and leaders in the Bartow County School System. Our success with the PLC process started with our system and local school guiding coalitions. Our school board supported our vision and were active participants within our PLC culture. The executive cabinet, Megan Brown, Macy Defnall, Lynn Huskins, and Clint Terza, ensured their departments supported our PLC mission, vision, and collective commitments.

We are so appreciative of Sharon Collum, Heather Carter, Amanda Creel, Mary Beth Stephens, Jennifer Mauldin, and Tania Amerson, who played instrumental roles in each step of our PLC implementation plan in the Bartow County School System.

In addition, we are grateful for the following Solution Tree associates: Jack Baldermann, Nicole Dimich, Cassandra Erkens, Emily Feltner, Angela Freese, Janel Keating, Jasmine Kullar, Mike Mattos, Rich Smith, Mandy Stalets, and Eric Twadell in teaching us as we grew in our understanding of the PLC process. We are so thankful to Claudia Wheatley and Douglas Rife for inspiring us to write this book. Thank you, Suzanne Kraszewski, our amazing editor, for your guidance and expertise along the way.

Solution Tree Press would like to thank the following reviewers:

Tonya Alexander
English Teacher (NBCT)
Owego Free Academy
Owego, New York

Molly Capps
Principal
McDeeds Creek Elementary School
Southern Pines, North Carolina

Jennifer Carr
Learning Director
Golden Hills Elementary School
Tehachapi, California

John Elkin
Assistant Superintendent
Center Point-Urbana CSD
Center Point, Iowa

John D. Ewald
Education Consultant
Frederick, Maryland

Jennifer LaBollita
Director, English Learner and World
  Language Programs
Revere Public Schools
Revere, Massachusetts

Peter Marshall
Education Consultant
Burlington, Ontario, Canada

Janel Ross
Principal
White River School District
Buckley, Washington

Christie Shealy
Director of Testing and Accountability
Anderson School District One
Williamston, South Carolina

Rea Smith
Math Facilitator
Rogers Public Schools
Rogers, Arkansas

Kim Timmerman
Principal
ADM Middle School
Adel, Iowa

Nadine Trépanier-Bisson
Director of Professional Learning
Ontario Principals' Council
Toronto, Ontario, Canada

John Unger
Superintendent
West Fork Schools
West Fork, Arkansas

Steven Weber
Associate Superintendent for Teaching
  and Learning
Fayetteville Public Schools
Fayetteville, Arkansas

Visit **go.SolutionTree.com/PLCbooks** to download the free reproducibles in this book.

Table of Contents

Reproducibles are in italics.

ABOUT THE AUTHORS xi

INTRODUCTION 1
Inspiring Innovation, Determination, and Motivation 2
Celebrating Commitment to the PLC Big Ideas 3
About This Book 5
Celebrating the Right Work 7

PART I: CULTURE SHIFTS AND CELEBRATION | 9

1 CELEBRATING FOR PLC TRANSFORMATION 11
Why Celebration? 12
How Should We Celebrate? 18

Conclusion 29
Chapter 1 Reflection Questions 30
Chapter 1 Journal Prompts 31

2 CELEBRATING AS A CATALYST FOR CHANGE 33
Ensuring Emotionally Healthy Competition 34
Planning for and Celebrating Productive Struggle 34
Celebrating Teammates 41
Celebrating Layers of Your PLC 42
Celebrating Collective Inquiry 44
Embracing Failure 47
Conclusion 49
Chapter 2 Reflection Questions 50
Chapter 2 Journal Prompts 52

3 LEVERAGING CELEBRATIONS IN YOUR LEADERSHIP . . . 55
Intentional Leadership in a PLC 56
Leading With a Guiding Coalition 60
Celebrating Guiding Coalition Leadership and
Monitoring the Plan Forward 73
Conclusion 74
Chapter 3 Reflection Questions 75
Chapter 3 Journal Prompts 76

PART II: CELEBRATION OF THE BIG IDEAS | 77

4 CELEBRATING A FOCUS ON LEARNING 79
Ensuring a Guaranteed and Viable Curriculum 79
Celebrating a Focus on Learning and the
Guaranteed and Viable Curriculum 81
Conclusion 91
Chapter 4 Reflection Questions 92
Chapter 4 Journal Prompts 93

5   CELEBRATING COLLABORATION AND COLLECTIVE RESPONSIBILITY 95

Celebrating a Collaborative Culture and Collective Responsibility   96

Conclusion 106

Chapter 5 Reflection Questions 107

Chapter 5 Journal Prompts 109

6   CELEBRATING RESULTS 111

Empowering Change Through Results 112

Turning Results Into Celebrations 118

Celebrating Results Through Tiers of Support 127

Celebrating Summative Results 132

Conclusion 140

Chapter 6 Reflection Questions 141

Chapter 6 Journal Prompts 142

EPILOGUE 143

REFERENCES AND RESOURCES 145

INDEX 149

About the Authors

David T. Chiprany, PhD, is the former deputy superintendent for the Bartow County School System in Georgia. He specializes in teaching and developing professional learning communities (PLCs) at the system, school, and team levels. He has served as an elementary school, middle school, and high school principal and is a college educational leadership coach and adjunct professor.

Dr. Chiprany has enjoyed leading and supporting the PLC culture shift in two school systems. During his tenure in the Bartow County School System, nineteen schools and the district earned Model PLC status. He has conducted many professional learning sessions on all areas of the PLC process. His audience has included teachers, principals, central office staff, board members, parents, and community members. Dr. Chiprany's presentations are filled with examples of actual PLC practices that were implemented at the local school and system level.

Working with the system guiding coalition, the Bartow County School System was recognized as a 2021 Model PLC school. The first year of their journey is captured in an article Dr. Chiprany coauthored with Phillip Page for the Winter 2020 issue of *AllThingsPLC Magazine* titled "A PLC Journey in the District Office." Professionally, Dr. Chiprany was awarded the 2008–2009 East Cobb Educator of the Year, Rotary Club of East Cobb, and the 2005–2006 Principal of the Year, Georgia PTA District 9.

Dr. Chiprany received his bachelor's degree in health and physical education from Kennesaw State University. He has a master's degree and specialist certification in educational leadership from the State University of West Georgia. He earned his PhD in educational leadership from the University of Southern Mississippi.

Phillip Page, EdD, is the former superintendent of the Bartow County School System in Georgia. His experience spans more than thirty-three years and includes serving as a biology teacher, high school assistant principal, middle school and high school principal, and assistant superintendent.

During his six years as superintendent, Dr. Page provided the support and leadership for the Bartow County School System to become a Model PLC at the district level and for nineteen of its schools to become Model PLC schools. He has been recognized as the Georgia PTA Middle School Principal of the Year and is a system recipient of the Leading-Edge award by the Georgia School Board Association. He has been twice named Citizen of the Year and twice nominated as State Superintendent of the Year.

Dr. Page earned a bachelor's degree in biology from the University of South Carolina, a master's degree in educational leadership from the University of South Florida, and a doctorate in educational leadership from the University of Sarasota.

To book David Chiprany or Phillip Page for professional development, contact pd@SolutionTree.com.

An excellent predictor of future behavior of any organization is to examine the people and events it elects to honor.

—Marcus Buckingham

Introduction

It is school board meeting night, but this meeting is not typical. The superintendent and board members of the Bartow County School System, a districtwide professional learning community (PLC), are recognizing a specific team with the High-Functioning Collaborative Team Award—the ultimate celebration of the PLC process within the district. Like all teams in a PLC, this high-functioning team is made up of members who work interdependently to achieve common goals that directly impact student achievement. They honor the collective commitments they have made to one another, creating an atmosphere of trust and mutual respect. They maintain a focus on learning, model a collaborative culture and collective responsibility, and remain results oriented (DuFour et al., 2024).

The team of teachers who will receive the award arrive with their families and friends, looking like they are attending a Broadway show. The team leader, a veteran teacher, often talks about how the PLC process made her a better teacher—even after twenty-five years in education. Another team member is in her fourth year of teaching and has never worked outside of the PLC process. She considers her team to be the reason for her success as an educator. The third member joined the team the previous year; he believes that transitioning to a new subject was much easier because of the team's established strong collaborative culture. The final member is a special education teacher. Her strength in specialized instruction benefits all the students the team teaches. The team is anxious but enthusiastic to have an opportunity to illustrate why their team is worthy of this highest recognition. They have spent the past week preparing their presentation to ensure it portrays the success of their team and students.

The school principal arrives with other teachers and staff. The deputy superintendent approaches the podium. He begins his remarks with words of admiration for the team of teachers, the school's guiding coalition, and their principal, who have worked collectively to ensure success for all students. The deputy superintendent reminds the board members and audience of the rigorous steps the collaborative team navigated to reach this level of success and celebration. He highlights how this team embraced each of the three big ideas of a PLC at Work (DuFour et al., 2024).

1. A focus on learning
2. A collaborative culture and collective responsibility
3. A results orientation

He praises the school's guiding coalition for fostering an environment that supports high-functioning collaborative teams, and he recognizes the principal for his professional learning leadership with the guiding coalition. Finally, the team is called to the podium to share how their teaching practices improved within a PLC, how their students' investment in learning increased through the PLC process, and most impressively, how their students demonstrated exceptional results in their levels of proficiency.

The team of teachers being celebrated on this evening produced their exceptional results during a time when educators were facing the challenge of educating students during a pandemic in which student performance was negatively impacted. The Nation's Report Card (National Center for Education Statistics, 2022) reports the following.

> A majority of states saw scores decline for fourth- and eighth-graders in mathematics and reading between 2019 and 2022. . . . The national average score declines in mathematics for fourth- and eighth-graders were the largest ever recorded in that subject.

The High-Functioning Collaborative Team Award is the highest award for collaborative teams within the district—a celebration of the totality of improved practices and results through a focus on learning, collaboration, and being results oriented. The team recognized that evening, along with the others recognized as high-functioning teams in previous similar celebratory events, is a team with the highest performance on state assessments and the most success in meeting the district's commitment to a guaranteed and viable curriculum—a curriculum that is aligned to standards, provided to every student, and teachable within the available amount of time (Marzano, 2019).

Inspiring Innovation, Determination, and Motivation

In your professional role, with whom do you identify in the school board's celebration of a high-functioning collaborative team? Are you the team member who is being celebrated for working interdependently with your teammates to learn from one another to achieve common goals directly impacting student achievement? Are you a member of the guiding coalition proudly watching your colleagues being recognized for their achievement producing exceptional results in student achievement? Are you the principal accepting the award as the leader of the school's guiding coalition for the in-depth professional learning you provided to the high-functioning collaborative team members? Or are you the deputy superintendent or superintendent recognizing and displaying what excellence looks like in a PLC? Regardless of your role, the inspiration a high-functioning collaborative team brings to a school and school district fuels the innovation, determination, and motivation required to establish collaborative teams focused on the right work to achieve uncommon results in teacher performance and student achievement.

Celebrating the right work is instrumental in stimulating the culture shifts in a PLC—the importance of going "from infrequent generic recognition to frequent specific recognition and a culture of celebration that creates many winners" (DuFour et al., 2024, p. 16). Currently, in its fifth year of the PLC process, the Bartow County School System has recognized many high-functioning collaborative teams at school board meetings. The frequency of recognition is key in inspiring others to strengthen their collaborative performance and apply for the award, which in turn supports the shift to becoming a Model PLC school system, a school system that has "effectively implemented all the essential elements of the PLC at Work process and has achieved multiple years of significant, sustained improvement in student achievement" (DuFour et al., 2024).

The process of identifying and recognizing high-functioning collaborative teams was inspired by Mike Mattos's (2015) *Are We a Group or a Team?* in which Mattos vividly describes the different attributes of 1, 5, and 10 teams. His portrayal captures the interdependent relationship and focuses on learning that high-functioning collaborative teams must have to be considered a 10 team. Mattos's work, additional supporting materials, and our own research were instrumental in developing celebrations for our district's high-functioning collaborative teams and guiding our district's schools in the backward design of their PLC.

The PLC journey is intentional and methodical, yet very personal. To achieve the desired exceptional results in teacher performance and student achievement, you must know where you're going and collectively build the roads and bridges to your destination. A close look at the success criteria for a high-functioning team reveals every practice, action, and behavior high-functioning collaborative teams exhibit to produce results in a PLC. This includes the creation of a guiding coalition to lead the PLC culture shift; when all collaborative teams have established norms, commitments, and SMART goals (strategic and specific, measurable, attainable, results oriented, and time bound); when the first collaborative team completes a teaching-assessing cycle; when a team implements Tier 2 interventions with improved proficiency for all students; and even when evidence shows a "doubter" becoming a champion of the PLC process. The key question PLCs should ask is, "What can we celebrate today?"

Celebrating Commitment to the PLC Big Ideas

Critical to the exceptional results Bartow County district has experienced are the Core Commitment Strands (see figure I.1, page 4), which detail the elements of a high-functioning collaborative team. In the spirit of Mattos's (2015) 1-5-10, the scoring for the rubric on each strand

CORE COMMITMENT 1: FOCUS ON LEARNING			
Strands	1 (Not true of our team)	5 (Our team is getting there)	10 (True of our team)
We have worked through the REAL process to determine readiness, endurance, assessment, and leverage to properly identify the essential standards for our subject area.			
We have identified appropriate learning targets with learning progressions as key components of the essential standard, and instructional planning is geared to ensure students meet proficiency including preventions, interventions, and reteaching.			
We have outlined the sequencing and pacing for each essential standard and illustrated our prevention, intervention, and reteaching strategies.			
We have developed our common summative assessments and corresponding common formative assessments establishing appropriate proficiency and depth of knowledge (DOK) levels through data-driven analysis.			
We use instructional techniques that are rigorous research-based strategies that foster high student performance on common summative assessments, MAP (Measures of Academic Progress) testing, Milestone assessments, and other assessment platforms.			

CORE COMMITMENT 2: COLLABORATIVE CULTURE AND COLLECTIVE RESPONSIBILITY			
Strands	1 (Not true of our team)	5 (Our team is getting there)	10 (True of our team)
We have identified team norms and protocols identifying student learning as a focus to guide us in working collaboratively.			
We have established a collegial environment where all members participate and have a connection and understanding of all our students we serve. Each member can articulate all aspects of the PLC process.			
We have established roles and responsibilities where all members have accountability toward student learning. Responsibilities are distributed to team members to address intervention and extension activities, and evidence of those implemented instructional strategies is observable.			
We have a pervasive culture of collaboratively evaluating student work, sharing effective instructional strategies, sharing what strategies did not work, and assessing prerequisite skills.			
When facing an obstacle of learning, collaboration, and results unique to our team, we develop strategies and processes to overcome the barriers.			

CORE COMMITMENT 3: RESULTS ORIENTATION			
Strands	1 (Not true of our team)	5 (Our team is getting there)	10 (True of our team)
We have analyzed student achievement and subgroup data, such as students with disabilities (SWD) and English speakers of other languages (ESOL), addressing gaps in performance. We have established SMART goals to improve upon the level of achievement we are working interdependently to attain. (Possible artifacts: SMART goals, unit plan, and data protocol)			
We can show growth using student learning proficiency data from common formative assessments and common summative assessments implemented through Tier 1 instruction and Tier 2 interventions throughout multiple teaching assessing cycles.			
We have evidence of instructional adjustments that led to increased student learning on common formative and common summative assessments.			
Our students play an active role in setting their learning goals and monitoring their results.			
We calibrate how we assess evidence of student learning while aligning rigor levels to district and state assessments.			

Figure I.1: Core commitment strands.

Visit ***go.SolutionTree.com/PLCbooks*** *for a free reproducible version of this figure.*

is a 1 (Not true of our team), 5 (Our team is getting there), or 10 (True of our team). There are three core commitments representing the three big ideas of a PLC: (1) a focus on learning, (2) a collaborative culture and collective commitments, and (3) a results orientation. Each core commitment contains five strands that illustrate a particular action that experts in the PLC process have deemed essential for highly effective teams to embody and implement (DuFour et al., 2024). Celebrating highly effective collaborative teams is just one of multiple strategies to foster a PLC culture shift in your school or school system. The second half of this book illustrates how celebrations play an important role in the implementation of the key concepts of the PLC three big ideas using the strands that appear in figure I.1.

About This Book

As the architects of the PLC process contend, "When celebrations continually remind people of the purpose and priorities of their organizations, members are more likely to embrace the purpose and work toward agreed-on priorities" (DuFour et al., 2024, p. 258). The focus of this book is to guide school leaders in developing their PLC culture shift through celebrating the right work of the PLC process.

Chapter 1, "Celebrating for PLC Transformation" (page 11), illustrates how celebrating even small wins is a powerful tool against resistors and doubters of the PLC process. Chapter 2, "Celebrating as a Catalyst for Change" (page 33), details the importance of publicly recognizing when teachers, through their collective ideas and decisions, improve instructional strategies and increase student learning and how this is a critical celebration tool in inspiring a PLC culture shift.

In chapter 3, "Leveraging Celebrations in Your Leadership" (page 55), the focus turns toward how the guiding coalition sets the environment at the system and local school for celebrations to occur and positively influence the PLC culture shift.

The next three chapters of the book illustrate how celebrations are critical to implementation of the key concepts of the three big ideas (DuFour et al., 2024). In chapter 4, "Celebrating a Focus on Learning" (page 79), tools and templates illustrate ways to celebrate answering PLC critical question one, "What do we want students to know and be able to do?" In chapter 5, "Celebrating Collaboration and Collective Responsibility" (page 95), multiple strategies guide schools through how to use monitoring tools of collaborative teams to identify small and large wins within collaboration. The chapter also illustrates how different platforms can publicly recognize the right work. In chapter 6, "Celebrating Results" (page 111), the power of celebrating growth in student learning shows how teachers, local school leaders, and central office staff play a role in celebrating student success. Throughout chapters 4–6, we discuss the High-Functioning Collaborative Team Award in detail as the ultimate celebration of the PLC process.

The conclusion of the book brings readers back to the board meeting portrayed in the introduction. Each member of the high-functioning collaborative team articulates how their team successfully implemented key actions of a focus on learning, collaboration and collective responsibility, and results orientation that led to their celebration.

Each chapter includes information on the why, explores the how, and presents templates and tools, reflective questions, and journal prompts. For a culture shift to occur, participants need to understand why this change is necessary. As Simon Sinek (2011) states, "People don't buy WHAT you do, they buy WHY you do it" (p. 45). For each chapter, research helps educators connect why celebration is a viable strategy as a catalyst for change and clarity of the right work. Research is a necessary tool in setting up an organization for accepting and implementing PLC processes.

In *The Knowing-Doing Gap: How Smart Companies Turn Knowledge Into Action*, Jeffrey Pfeffer and Robert I. Sutton (2000) point out that one of the main obstacles organizations face is that they equate talking about something with actually taking action. In our work, we find that many schools understand and have talked about the importance of celebration but do not know how to celebrate. Going from the why to the how is a big step in the change process. Each chapter presents exemplars on how local and system leaders put the why into action through collaboratively developed practices where celebration events move the school or system from theory to practice.

Templates and tools are designed for the reader to use immediately. However, in the spirit of the collaborative process, we encourage leaders to work with their guiding coalitions to ensure the templates and tools meet the needs of staff and to make any adjustments to the templates or tools as appropriate for the school or system.

As philosopher and psychologist John Dewey is often quoted as saying, "We do not learn from experience . . . we learn from reflecting on experience." Additionally, in *Leading From Within: Building Organizational Leadership Capacity*, David Kolzow (2014) states, "Self-reflection is an important behavior that is demonstrated by leaders. . . . For leaders to take their followers in a good direction, they really need to take the time to reflect and learn from their experiences" (p. 69). Readers will have the opportunity to take the knowledge from each chapter and their experiences and discuss how to apply it within their school or system. The reflective questions are tailored to the context of the chapter, and we encourage the members of the guiding coalition to work through the questions collectively. Reflection on a school's current reality regarding celebrations is an important step in building a culture of celebration.

A guided journal will provide prompts or questions at the end of each chapter. These prompts are intended for you to personalize the content and initiate what works for you personally into your professional environment. The advantages of journaling as a part of reflection range from encouraging self-confidence, to boosting emotional intelligence, to assisting in your pursuit of goals and academic growth (University of St. Augustine for Health Sciences, 2020). According to Margie Meacham (2021):

> Keeping a journal is a reflective learning activity that requires the writer to consider what they've learned, explore how they feel about the content, connect it to previous learning, and capture any questions they may have. Several studies have discovered these benefits, when a journal is used in combination to any other learning modality: retention over time, deeper understanding of the content, application of the content to real-world problems, and expressed interest and learner engagement.

Celebrating the Right Work

Celebration of the right work—the three big ideas—within the PLC process remains a driving force in our school system and at local schools. We began celebrating the small wins as our system guiding coalition designed and put into practice our PLC implementation timeline. As we accomplished each step in our journey, we purposely and frequently celebrated exemplars from within our school system. The celebrations were captured at the local school level, at the system level, in board meetings, and through social media. Celebration was a major factor in over half of our schools being recognized as Model PLC schools. We are excited to share in the following chapters how celebration will move your school or school system to being a high-functioning PLC.

PART I

CULTURE SHIFTS AND CELEBRATION

An effective celebration program will convince every staff member that they can be a winner and that their efforts can be noted and appreciated.

—Richard DuFour, Robert Eaker, Rebecca DuFour, Thomas W. Many, Mike Mattos, and Anthony Muhammad

CHAPTER 1

Celebrating for PLC Transformation

In the introduction, we described the most celebratory event in the Bartow County School System's districtwide PLC—presentation of the High-Functioning Collaborative Team Award—when school board members, district administrators, and the winning school's principal, guiding coalition, collaborative team, and family, friends, and colleagues gather to celebrate the team's extraordinary results. This locally televised event, which is also chronicled in the local newspaper and on all the school district's social media sites, clearly indicates what the school district values as the right work. This celebration provides evidence of the PLC culture shift embedded in the collaborative team, in the school's guiding coalition, and among all staff. It is a celebration available to every collaborative team in the school district but awarded only to those teams demonstrating effective teamwork through collaboration, support for a guaranteed and viable curriculum, and evidence of all students learning on or above grade level through effective initial instruction and systematic interventions and extensions.

In the first year of PLC implementation, only a few collaborative teams within a school will likely rise to this level of recognition. However, publicly celebrating their success motivates other teams throughout the district to trust in the PLC process and reach out for advice on how to improve. The celebrated teams become ambassadors of the PLC culture shift and, in turn, provide best practices for other teams to become celebrated. This is indeed a powerful and transformative celebration showcasing the learning progressions of each team through their PLC journey as well as a valuable opportunity for each team member to share their growth within the PLC process and offer a personal testimony of how student success would not be possible without their teammates.

There is admiration from the audience as team members describe the power of their collaboration in driving Tier 1 (best first) instruction to higher levels, allowing more students to be proficient on the end-of-unit assessment and therefore able to extend their learning during the school's designated Tier 2 intervention time. The excitement of the presentation always culminates with the sharing of positive results in student achievement (like graphs showing student proficiency with each essential standard, proficiency after Tier 2 interventions, and examples of student investment in their success) that identify what is possible when a collaborative team embraces the defining attributes of a PLC.

The school board's celebration of this collaborative team highlights the importance of effective collaboration in making the adults better academic leaders, the intentionality of looking at data and discussing the instructional practices that led to the student results, and the power of collective teacher efficacy to ensure all students are proficient on the identified essential standards. The school board's celebration epitomizes everything a school district promotes as being the right work in a PLC. To be recognized for this illustrious award, collaborative teams must demonstrate they are practicing what is "tight" or required, non-negotiable in the PLC process. The school board's celebration of these highly effective teams of teachers serves as an example for others to unequivocally recognize how improving teaching practices by working together with collective responsibility for student learning always delivers positive results for students. There are no teachers who cannot achieve this highest recognition.

All PLCs can produce extraordinary results for student achievement. John Hattie's (Nottingham, 2018) research shows that collective teacher efficacy, teacher estimates of achievement, response to intervention (RTI), deliberate practice, and providing timely feedback all have high effect sizes on student achievement. These are all fundamental objectives of the PLC process. Together, these practices have an effect size of 1.128 standard deviations on student achievement. That is almost three years of student academic achievement.

Why Celebration?

Neuroscience shows the human spirit craves a winning experience (Robertson, 2012), which is why every recognition and celebration must have clear success criteria that every team of teachers can achieve. The success criteria promote the work within a PLC that the district and school value with clear evidence of high achievement for all students. The school board recognition showcases the collaborative team's practices as being successful, provides an example of work strategies for other collaborative teams to learn from and collaborate with on their journey to becoming a higher-functioning team, and, most importantly, reinforces to all staff the PLC process produces exceptional results of all students becoming proficient on the established guaranteed and viable curriculum.

In *The Progress Principle*, Teresa M. Amabile and Steven J. Kramer (2011) explain how "people are more creative and productive when they are deeply engaged in the work, when they feel happy, and when they think highly of their projects, coworkers, managers, and organizations. When people enjoy consistently positive inner work lives, they are also more committed to their work and more likely to work well with colleagues" (p. 3).

With research showing a decline in the number of teachers staying in education and a decrease in the number of teachers entering the profession (Jotkoff, 2022), it is imperative we begin to acknowledge the impact clear and meaningful celebrations have on validating the work of teachers and other instructional staff. Some people prefer to be celebrated with thousands of people in attendance, others prefer a more intimate celebration, and, to some people, a handwritten note of appreciation has the greatest impact. Just as winning shouldn't be relegated to a once-a-year opportunity, neither should the opportunity to be celebrated. Where there are winning moments, there are celebratory moments. Daily, weekly, monthly, and yearly wins allow for daily, weekly, monthly, and yearly celebrations. If we take the time to look, there are legitimate and sincere wins and celebrations all around us.

According to Gert-Jan Pepping and colleagues (2010), an individual's outward expression of success through immediate celebration directly impacts their teammates. Specifically, "the celebratory behaviours displaying pride had a positive impact on teammates" (p. 988). This research provides clarity on the power of celebration and its effect on prioritizing the "right work" of an organization and creating opportunities for all employees to have winning moments with their peers.

When organizations initiate a culture shift, there are always those who embrace the new expectations and look forward to learning and experimenting to find better outcomes. Unfortunately, there are also doubters and resisters. In *Transforming School Culture*, Anthony Muhammad (2018) describes four types of staff members.

1. **Believers:** Those who are "willing and able" to embrace change, self-reflect, and possess a determination to personally contribute to improvement leading to student outcomes

2. **Tweeners:** Those who are "willing but unable" due to a lack of skill sets but who are open, optimistic, and ready to learn

3. **Survivors:** Those who are "unwilling but able" due to a sense of hopelessness and struggle to see anything that could make a positive impact

4. **Fundamentalists:** Those who are "unwilling and unable" because they care more about their personal outcomes than team goals or aspirations and resist change due to a threat to their autonomy

We will discuss in chapter 3 (page 55) how to identify these four types of staff members in your organization, how to leverage your leadership to create positive experiences for the doubters, and how to minimize the negative impact of the resisters on your PLC culture shift.

For organizations seeking to change behaviors and priorities, celebrating the success in the new paradigm is essential for rewarding the employees who embraced the change process, convincing doubters to see that the new process produces better results, and minimizing or silencing the resisters who consistently share with other employees how the "new way" will not be effective.

When we visit schools, we often ask the principal to share the school's best celebration. We do this partly to learn the best celebratory practices to share with others but also to gauge if the "best" school or district celebration connects to learning. Unfortunately, in many schools, the best celebrations do not remind people of the purpose and priority of the school—learning. In a discussion with one school, the principal enthusiastically shared how each month, the staff member who logged the most steps on their fitness watch won an award. The principal outlined the rules of the competition, noted how many staff members were participating, named the last three staff members to win the award, and proudly gave an example of how it was impacting the staff by the increased number of teachers walking the halls or outside track during their planning period and lunch. While we acknowledge the importance of celebrations to improve school climate, recognize personal accomplishments, and promote healthy habits, we also know what you celebrate is the perception of what you value most in your school or district.

Celebrating District or School Staff

In a PLC, school leaders will encounter doubters and resisters of the culture shift. Though there will be struggles, there will be many early small wins for staff and students. Be ready to capitalize on the wins of district and school staff to ensure the doubters begin to believe and the resisters are no longer the loudest voices in the room. Figure 1.1 details the expected wins early in the PLC process. Use this chart to plan how and when you will celebrate these successes.

PLANNING FOR CELEBRATIONS WORKSHEET	
Directions: Plan how you will monitor and celebrate the early wins in your PLC.	
Win: You have chosen the members of your first guiding coalition to lead the PLC culture shift.	
Monitor:	Celebrate:
Win: The guiding coalition has held their first meeting and committed to PLC transformation.	
Monitor:	Celebrate:
Win: The guiding coalition has achieved its first consensus on a change in practice or policy to remove a barrier.	
Monitor:	Celebrate:
Win: The guiding coalition holds the first staff professional learning day.	
Monitor:	Celebrate:

Win: All team members understand why they are together and understand the meaning behind their collaboration	
Monitor:	Celebrate:

Win: All collaborative teams have established norms, commitments, and SMART goals.	
Monitor:	Celebrate:

Win: Collaborative teams have met their first SMART goal.	
Monitor:	Celebrate:

Win: A collaborative team has completed a teaching-assessing cycle (the first team to do so) with Tier 2 interventions and improved proficiency for all students.	
Monitor:	Celebrate:

Win: There is evidence of a doubter becoming a champion of the PLC process.	
Monitor:	Celebrate:

Win: We have established Tier 2 intervention and extension into the master schedule.	
Monitor:	Celebrate:

Win: What can we celebrate today?	
Monitor:	Celebrate:

Figure 1.1: Planning for celebrations worksheet.

*Visit **go.SolutionTree.com/PLCbooks** for a free reproducible version of this figure.*

One of the first wins to celebrate PLC transformation is the selection of the guiding coalition to lead the PLC work for your district or school. This process must be carefully conducted and monitored to ensure the assembly of the most influential staff members to initiate the culture shift through their learning, the facilitation of shared knowledge to others, and collective inquiry to solve problems. Chapter 3 provides a monitoring tool (page 55) to assist in the selection of your first guiding coalition members. This tool ensures you begin your journey with the strongest guiding coalition to lead the staff. In turn, celebrate them not as a coronation, but instead with an outward expression of gratitude to acknowledge the accepted responsibility required to build a culture of collective leadership and teacher efficacy. Be transparent in their responsibilities and grateful for their commitment.

A second win, for example, occurs when your guiding coalition plans for and executes its first staff professional learning day. This day shows the transformation from outside staff dictating the learning outcomes to the guiding coalition creating the learning outcomes based on feedback from staff. The monitoring for this day often begins with a survey to staff on what they need for clarity, skill development, or support within the three big ideas of a PLC: a focus on learning, collaboration and collective responsibility, and results orientation (DuFour et al., 2024). Once the results from the survey are analyzed, the guiding coalition plans for the day by deciding who will lead each session topic.

To enhance collective teacher efficacy, it is recommended that, when possible, members of the guiding coalition lead the sessions. However, inviting central office support staff or educational consultants to assist in professional learning is powerful if the school staff knows the plan was created by the guiding coalition. Once the day is complete, the celebration is the acknowledgment in front of the school staff of a meaningful day of targeted learning in the areas they indicated were most important to their growth as instructional leaders. Targeted outward acknowledgment and praise of the staff for providing the survey feedback and for the guiding coalition members in planning the day provides the intrinsic satisfaction and builds the collective leader and teacher efficacy required for the PLC culture shift.

For collaborative team celebration, figure 1.1 provides specific wins related to implementing collaborative work in a PLC; for example, celebrate when all teams have established norms, when all teams have met their first SMART goal, and when a team completes a teaching-assessing cycle and implements interventions successfully to improve student proficiency. School and district leaders can personalize the chart for their own celebrations, ensuring that the celebration is directly connected to student learning, shows evidence of success in one of the three big ideas (focus on learning, collaborative culture and collective responsibility, and focus on results). Consider what you can add to the chart as an anticipated action item to celebrate. Will it continue to build collective leader or teacher efficacy?

Celebrating District or School Office Personnel

In our work with superintendents, the conversation around celebrations always gravitates to what the schools are doing. When pressed to name the best celebration the school district has for staff members, the superintendent usually answers with the Teacher of the Year banquet. This expected and typical answer opens the door for a conversation regarding what is the best celebration the district office has for district office personnel. Too often, there is silence. Every district office staff member has a link to student achievement by directly impacting the employees who work with the students each day. We often forget to connect how each person in the central office impacts the success and winning of the local schools.

Few people immediately name a district's technology director or the specialists who serve the local schools as an integral part of a school's academic success. However, walk the halls of any school when the internet is not working, and you will see a school unable to function. Technology directors and specialists take pride in their work, but when a superintendent or principal directly connects their work to successful classroom instruction and student learning, there is a different approach to their work. Another example is the purchasing specialist in the finance department. This position's typical responsibilities include ordering teacher supplies, equipment, and other essentials for the teacher to both provide quality instruction and improve practices through professional development. This person is critical to ensuring each teacher is prepared to provide the quality instruction necessary for all students to learn on or above grade level.

To validate how each district office employee impacts student achievement, use figure 1.2 to highlight each person's direct or indirect positive impact on teachers and students in the local schools. For many district office employees, this will be the first time they clearly see how their roles and responsibilities impact the celebrated student achievement of the schools. This chart allows the superintendent or other central office leadership to celebrate the staff who are often forgotten but are just as worthy of recognition as the local school staff.

CELEBRATING THE DISTRICT OFFICE PERSONNEL				
Office:				Team leader:
Department:				Team members:
How does this office impact student learning?	List two ways the department supports collaboration.	List two new innovative ideas of this department.	List two positive influences of this department.	List two extraordinary results of this department.

Figure 1.2: Celebrating the district or school office personnel's contribution to learning.

*Visit **go.SolutionTree.com/PLCbooks** for a free reproducible version of this figure.*

We encourage district office leaders to envision the central office staff as they would a local school staff. How do you collectively show appreciation for their work? How often do you bring them together to celebrate? The first step is to create a subcommittee with representatives from each central office division. Representation from finance, human resources, technology, communications, academics, and so on empowers each department to invest in the celebratory process.

In one Model PLC school district, the celebration subcommittee created the three ideas of (1) innovation, (2) positive influence, and (3) collaboration to drive the work connecting all central office divisions in the district. A celebration board in the commons area of the district office provides a place for employees to recognize their peers when they are seen demonstrating behaviors in one or more of these three ideas. At the end of each month, more than seventy district office staff members come together in the board room to celebrate the monthly accomplishments. During this scheduled time, employees are recognized for the innovative, positive, or collaborative work for which they were acknowledged on the three ideas board. Just as teachers often get notes from students or parents expressing gratitude for their positive influence, this simple celebration created by a subcommittee of employees provides the same message "You make a positive impact on our work—Thank you!" Most teachers keep a file or box of these uplifting messages from students and parents; the district office staff in this school district keeps these recognition cards taped to their walls, on their desks, or beside their computer monitors. Like with teachers, these small gestures of appreciation remind central office staff that their behaviors, actions, and efforts are noticed and appreciated. They are also a reminder of the power of collective efficacy in our work.

How Should We Celebrate?

Celebrations should be targeted and meaningful. Without input from those being celebrated, good intentions may result in poor outcomes. Consider the following example of a principal attempting to reward a student for coming to school each day. At this school, when a student would get to ten days of absences, an administrator or counselor would assume the responsibility of motivating the student to change their attendance behavior. The principal met with one student who had twelve absences with twenty days left in the school year. He offered the student a season pass to an amusement park in the area if he did not miss another day of school. The principal's intention was admirable, but his logic was flawed.

After attending school on the following day, the student was absent for the next two days. The principal summoned the student for a stern lecture and to express his disappointment. After several minutes of a one-sided conversation, the exasperated principal simply asked, "How could you miss school with such a generous offer of a season pass to an amusement park? I just don't understand how it didn't motivate you to come to school for the next twenty days."

Lifting his head toward the principal, the student replied, "That pass doesn't do anything for me. I don't have any way to get there, and my parents wouldn't let me go even if I had a ride." Feeling ashamed for the harsh lecture, the principal asked, "So what would it take for you to come to school for the next seventeen days?" Without much thought, the student asked if he could have a Yoo-hoo drink on Fridays if he didn't miss a day during the week. Surprised and speechless, the principal nodded his head as the student left his office. For the next three Fridays, the principal delivered two Yoo-hoo drinks to the students who did not miss another day of school.

There are multiple lessons in this story, but let's focus on the lesson regarding celebrations. The principal's intention was admirable as he tried to extrinsically motivate and celebrate the student's positive behavior in attending school. The logic was flawed, however, because the principal assumed a season pass to an amusement park would be exciting to the student. The principal never included the student in the celebration process, which led to frustration and delayed results. In a PLC, student attendance would have been a barrier hindering student achievement, and a guiding coalition subcommittee made up of staff and students would have looked at solutions to overcome the attendance barrier. Along with the subcommittee of staff and students identifying causes of poor attendance within their specific student population, they also have the student voice to share the motivators for students to commit to attending school.

Through the subcommittee's work and recommendation, the principal, administrators, and counselors would have been given a developed and vetted plan to attack the attendance problem. Instead, the principal, assistant principals, and counselors were working in isolation to solve a significant problem. Isolation is an enemy in a PLC. Whenever isolation exists, extraordinary results rarely exist; however, when isolation is removed and collaboration occurs, extraordinary results are not far behind.

Creating celebrations should be the responsibility of a guiding coalition subcommittee to ensure ownership of what is celebrated and how. The use of subcommittees for collective inquiry and recommendations ensures collective leader and teacher efficacy throughout the PLC process.

Create Opportunities for Small Wins

Often, we think of celebrations as big events. Annually, we celebrate the Teacher of the Year, Classified Employee of the Year, and Volunteer of the Year. However, Richard DuFour (2004) states these are the worst celebrations we have in a school and district. These one-time events create one winner per school and leave everyone else as a loser. In many cases, the one winner doesn't represent the best employee in the area of student learning. Instead, the award is given for reasons unrelated to positive results in student achievement. DuFour encourages educational leaders to create small wins and celebrations that every employee can achieve—celebrations that continually recognize the work we would want every employee to exhibit to improve student learning.

In our work, we see the greatest satisfaction in all staff when the school celebrations encompass both formative and summative celebrations.

- *Formative* celebrations are the small celebrations that occur daily during collaboration meetings, a visit from a school leader during Tier 1 instruction, or the success of an activity during extension time.

- *Summative* celebrations are the schoolwide celebrations recognized in front of the entire staff and posted on social media. These celebrations may include all collaborative teams who met their essential standard's SMART goals, achieved 95 percent or greater student proficiency on the essential standard after Tier 2 interventions, beat the state average and improved results on a state assessment, or achieved school board recognition status.

Celebrations in a PLC require the same attention to detail and intentionality as the other foundational PLC transformational pieces. Successful celebrations announce to everyone, "This is working. Let's go!" Just as it is critical to show student work examples that meet and exceed the standard, it is also critical to show teachers what the right work looks like in the PLC process. In our work, the most powerful professional learning occurs when teachers work with their peers to improve instruction. It is the catalyst for high-functioning collaborative teams, and it's equally effective with school staff training. When teachers who have been celebrated for extraordinary results provide the professional learning for their peers, you are essentially "celebrating a celebration" while showing all teachers what proficiency looks like in getting extraordinary results for teacher performance and student achievement.

For example, the Bartow County School System celebrates its high-functioning teams in three ways.

1. Local school faculty meeting
2. School board meeting
3. Showcasing them at the summer orientation for new teachers

During the orientation, new teachers choose four sessions to attend. Each session opens with the celebrated team's journey from their focus on teaching and working independently to their focus on learning and working interdependently. The new teachers observe how each team uses the four critical questions of a PLC (DuFour et al., 2024) to ensure proficiency for all students on the guaranteed and viable curriculum and to show how the PLC process creates a positive learning environment for both adults and students.

1. What knowledge, skills, and dispositions should every student acquire as a result of this unit, this course, or this grade level?
2. How will we know when each student has acquired the essential knowledge and skills?
3. How will we respond when some students do not learn?
4. How will we extend the learning for students who are already proficient? (p. 44)

After attending the sessions, new teachers often express how each team's journey was different but still centered on the three big ideas—focus on learning, collaboration and collective responsibility, and focus on results—how each team had a different personality but produced the same positive results for student achievement, and how they learned so much that was never taught in college or in their previous school district.

By "celebrating the celebrations," the high-functioning teams ensure new teachers know what is expected in every classroom and as part of a collaborative team. It is the perfect introduction to the school culture that fosters collective teacher efficacy and responsibility to drive Tier 1 instruction, Tier 2 intervention, and Tier 3 reteaching to produce extraordinary results for teachers and students.

Determine Your Current Reality

Whether you are just beginning your PLC journey, relaunching your PLC journey, or refining your PLC process, it is important to use celebrations when identifying your current reality during your PLC culture shift. DuFour and colleagues (2024) chart out what the culture of a school looks like when it functions as a PLC compared to a traditional school. As Robert Eaker and Janel Keating (2008) state in "A Shift in School Culture," not all PLCs look alike, but all reflect three critical cultural shifts: (1) a shift in the fundamental purpose from teaching to learning, (2) a shift in the work of teachers, and (3) a shift in focus.

- According to Eaker and Keating (2008), "Professional learning communities shift their primary purpose, their reason for being, from a *focus on teaching to a focus on learning*" (p. 15). This shift requires a different mindset from the traditional expectation of presenting content using individual teacher-created assessments to measure learning during a fixed time in the unit of study to a mindset of determining what is most essential for students to learn and creating common assessments to measure how well students are learning and what interventions are needed to reach a level of proficiency.

- The *shift in the work of teachers* in PLCs centers on the idea that "there is no hope of helping all students learn unless those within the school work collaboratively in a collective effort to achieve that fundamental purpose" (Eaker & Keating, 2008, p. 15). The traditional environment of teachers working in isolation with responsibility for their students to learn is replaced with the expectation of teachers collaborating in meaningful teams to take responsibility for all students learning the essential skills and content.

- Finally, the *shift in focus of educators* in PLCs recognizes the following.

    > [Educators] will not know if their collaborative efforts to help all students learn have been successful without a fixation on results. They are hungry for evidence of student learning, and they use that evidence both to respond to students who need additional time and support as well as to inform and improve their professional practice. (Eaker & Keating, 2008, p. 15)

It is within these fundamental shifts in culture that schools must routinely evaluate their current reality, engage the guiding coalition to embrace solutions to identified barriers, and celebrate each small win through evidence of success.

Use figure 1.3 (page 22) to determine your current reality relating to the cultural shifts in a PLC. By using this tool, you and your leadership team can identify the areas where your PLC is most effective and celebrate those aspects of your culture. It is critical to show your staff that you're not discarding everything they're doing and "starting over." The right-hand column in each section of the survey represents the culture shift necessary to fully realize the empowerment teachers and leaders gain with PLC transformation. Once you have completed the survey, celebrate with your staff where your current reality indicates a 5, and celebrate the 3s by identifying the specific areas where the best practice is occurring. Use the identified 1s and 3s to work with your guiding coalition or leadership team to develop a strategic plan to determine which actions are needed to move the 1s to 3s and the 3s to 5s, as discussed in the next section.

CULTURAL SHIFTS IN A PLC SURVEY TOOL

Directions: Use the following rating scale to indicate the extent to which each statement is true of your school.

Rating Key: 1 = Not evident; 3 = Evident in isolated areas; 5 = Evident in most areas

A Shift in Fundamental Purpose

From	To	Rating
A focus on teaching	A focus on learning	
An emphasis on what was taught	A fixation on what students learned	
Coverage of content	Demonstration of proficiency	
Providing individual teachers with curriculum documents such as state standards and curriculum guides	Engaging collaborative teams in building shared knowledge regarding essential curricula	
Expecting some students to learn	Expecting all students to learn	

A Shift in Use of Assessments

From	To	Rating
Infrequent summative assessments	Frequent common formative assessments	
Assessments to determine which students failed to learn by the deadline	Assessments to identify students who need additional time and support	
Assessments used to reward and punish students	Assessments used to inform and motivate students	
Assessing many things infrequently	Assessing a few things frequently	
Individual teacher assessments	Collaborative team-developed assessments	
Each teacher determining the criteria to be used in assessing student work	Collaborative teams clarifying the criteria and ensuring consistency among team members when assessing student work	
An overreliance on one kind of assessment	Balanced assessments	
Focusing on average scores	Monitoring each student's proficiency in every essential skill	

A Shift in the Response When Students Don't Learn

From	To	Rating
Individual teachers determining the appropriate response	Systematic response that ensures support for every student	
Fixed time and support for learning	Time and support for learning as variables	
Remediation	Intervention	
Invitational support outside of the school day	Directed (that is, required) support occurring during the school day	
One opportunity to demonstrate learning	Multiple opportunities to demonstrate learning	

A Shift in the Work of Teachers

From	To	Rating
Isolation	Collaboration	
Each teacher clarifying what students must learn	Collaborative teams building shared knowledge and understanding about essential learning	
Each teacher assigning priority to different learning standards	Collaborative teams establishing the priority of respective learning standards	

Each teacher determining the pacing of the curriculum	Collaborative teams of teachers agreeing on common pacing	
Individual teachers attempting to discover ways to improve results	Collaborative teams of teachers helping each other improve	
Privatization of practice	Open sharing of practice	
Decisions made based on individual preferences	Decisions made collectively by building shared knowledge of best practice	
"Collaboration lite" on matters unrelated to student achievement	Collaboration explicitly focused on issues and questions that most impact student achievement	
An assumption that these are "my students, those are your students"	An assumption that these are "our students"	
A Shift in Focus		
From	To	Rating
An external focus on issues outside the school	An internal focus on steps the staff can take to improve the school	
A focus on inputs	A focus on results	
A focus on a student's background	A focus on the student's future (potential)	
Goals related to completion of projects and activities	SMART goals demanding evidence of student learning	
Teachers gathering data from their individually constructed tests to assign grades	Collaborative teams acquiring information from common assessments to (1) inform their individual and collective practice, and (2) respond to students who need additional time and support	
A Shift in School Culture		
From	To	Rating
Independence	Interdependence	
A language of complaint	A language of commitment	
Long-term strategic planning	Planning for short-term wins	
Infrequent generic recognition	Frequent specific recognition and a culture of celebration that creates many winners	
A Shift in Professional Development		
From	To	Rating
External training (workshops and courses)	Job-embedded learning	
The expectation that learning occurs infrequently (on the few days devoted to professional development)	An expectation that learning is ongoing and occurs as part of routine work practice	
Presentations to entire faculties	Team-based action research	
Learning by listening	Learning by doing	
Learning individually through courses and workshops	Learning collectively by working together	
Assessing impact based on teacher satisfaction ("Did you like it?")	Assessing impact based on evidence of improved student learning	

Source: Adapted from DuFour et al., 2024.

Figure 1.3: Cultural shifts in a PLC survey tool.

*Visit **go.SolutionTree.com/PLCbooks** for a free reproducible version of this figure.*

Create a Culture Shift Strategic Plan

At Cass High School, the data from their culture shifts survey reflected an undesirable current reality: the school did not provide a systematic approach for teachers to respond to students who did not show proficiency on end-of-unit assessments. To address this issue, the school's guiding coalition used the strategic planning document in figure 1.4 to create a blueprint to shift the school's response when students didn't learn an essential standard the first time. Cass High School identified the plan in figure 1.5 (page 28) for shifting their response when students don't learn.

PLC CULTURE SHIFT STRATEGIC PLAN	
Directions: Using the cultural shifts in a PLC survey (figure 1.3, page 22), divide your guiding coalition or leadership team into seven subcommittees representing the different sections of the survey. Each subcommittee should begin the collective inquiry process to determine what is needed to move the identified 1s to 3s and the identified 3s to 5s. Once the subcommittee has developed a plan, they should present it to the full guiding coalition or leadership team for consensus.	
A Shift in Fundamental Purpose	
From:	To:
List any barriers preventing this shift in culture:	
What professional development is needed for the staff?	
How will we monitor progress?	
How will we celebrate progress?	
A Shift in Use of Assessments	
From:	To:
List any barriers preventing this shift in culture:	

What professional development is needed for the staff?

How will we monitor progress?

How will we celebrate progress?

A Shift in the Response When Students Don't Learn	
From:	To:
List any barriers preventing this shift in culture:	

What professional development is needed for the staff?

How will we monitor progress?

How will we celebrate progress?

A Shift in the Work of Teachers	
From:	To:
List any barriers preventing this shift in culture:	

Figure 1.4: PLC culture shift strategic plan.

continued →

What professional development is needed for the staff?

How will we monitor progress?

How will we celebrate progress?

A Shift in Focus

From:	To:

List any barriers preventing this shift in culture:

What professional development is needed for the staff?

How will we monitor progress?

How will we celebrate progress?

A Shift in School Culture

From:	To:

List any barriers preventing this shift in culture:

What professional development is needed for the staff?

How will we monitor progress?

How will we celebrate progress?

A Shift in Professional Development

From:	To:

List any barriers preventing this shift in culture:

What professional development is needed for the staff?

How will we monitor progress?

How will we celebrate progress?

*Visit **go.SolutionTree.com/PLCbooks** for a free reproducible version of this figure.*

A SHIFT IN THE RESPONSE WHEN STUDENTS DON'T LEARN	
From:	To:
Fixed time and support for learning focused on remediation, invitational support outside of the school day, and one opportunity to demonstrate learning.	A systematic response that ensures support for every student including time and support for learning as variables, intervention on specific learning targets within the essential standard, and directed support occurring during the school day with multiple opportunities to demonstrate learning.
List any barriers preventing this shift in culture:	
Time in the school day for targeted interventions, teachers regrouping and sharing students to provide interventions by student, by target, and the opportunity for students to improve their academic grade to reflect improved learning.	
What professional development is needed for the staff?	
Learning by Doing (DuFour et al., 2024) chapter 8 Case Study (p. 197) and Here's How (p. 199) information; *Taking Action* (Buffum, Mattos, & Malone, 2018) study guide; research Model PLC schools and how they developed a system of intervention (visit AllThingsPLC.info); RTI at Work Institute Standards-Based Learning in Action workshop.	
How will we monitor progress?	
Use the "Professional Learning Communities at Work Continuum: Providing Students With Systematic Interventions and Extensions" in *Learning by Doing* (DuFour et al., 2024, p. 213) to provide evidence of movement between pre-initating and sustaining stage. Retake the cultural shifts in a PLC survey (figure 1.3, page 22) at the end of the semester to gain insight into the staff's perception of growth and improvement.	
How will we celebrate progress?	
Highlight growth and improvement at a faculty meeting and include these results in the quarterly school newsletter. Identify and praise the subcommittee members responsible for the intervention schedule. Invite superintendent and other district office staff to observe and give recognition to staff.	

Source: Cass High School, White, Georgia. Used with permission.
Figure 1.5: Cass High School's PLC culture shift strategic plan.

Visit **go.SolutionTree.com/PLCbooks** *for a free reproducible version of this figure.*

Using the PLC culture shift strategic plan (figure 1.5) allowed the Cass High School guiding coalition to define the barrier preventing increased learning for all students after an end-of-unit assessment and to begin collective inquiry into a systematic response that ensures support for every student by learning target within an essential standard. This intentional focus spurred the Cass High School staff to create a Tier 2 intervention and extension block of time within their daily bell schedule to support all students who needed additional time and support for learning within the essential standards. It also provided time for a quality extension of learning for students who demonstrated proficiency on their end-of-unit assessment. For the first time, teachers at Cass High School gave students the priority and support necessary to ensure they were not falling behind if they didn't learn it the first time. This targeted support resulted in Cass High School celebrating an increased graduation rate for their students with disabilities from 69 percent in 2020 to 92 percent in 2022.

Conclusion

Neuroscience shows us that people crave winning experiences (Robertson, 2012). School leaders can create such experiences for school and district staff undergoing PLC transformation by creating opportunities for recognition and celebration. To do so, school leaders must provide clear criteria for what success looks like and recognition opportunities that showcase collaborative teams' successful practices. These winning experiences also provide examples of work strategies for other collaborative teams to learn from on their journey to becoming a higher functioning team. Most importantly, celebrations reinforce to all staff that the PLC process produces exceptional results.

This chapter identified the need to celebrate district and school staff and office personnel for small wins that are both formative and summative, and it provided tools for determining current reality and planning the cultural shifts necessary in PLC transformation so teams can plan celebration strategically. Use the reflection questions (page 30) to reflect on the celebrations that occur currently in your school or district and what these say about what you value. Then, consider what celebrations you can add to support teams engaged in the work of a PLC. In the journal prompt questions (page 31), reflect on your personal views about celebration.

The next chapter examines celebrating as a catalyst for change and how productive struggle followed by celebration can help teams in PLCs achieve exceptional results.

Chapter 1 Reflection Questions

Reflect on the following questions from an organizational viewpoint.

1. List the celebrations occurring in your school and school district.

2. Which of these celebrations are formative celebrations?

3. Which of these celebrations are summative celebrations?

4. Which, if any, celebrations indicate to a visitor what you value most in teachers?

5. Who determines what you are celebrating and how it is celebrated?

6. List the celebrations to add to your school or district to signify what the right work is and who is engaged in the right work of a PLC.

Chapter 1 Journal Prompts

Reflect on these questions from a personal viewpoint.

1. What recognition or celebration has meant the most to you personally?

2. What recognition or celebration has meant the most to you professionally?

3. Who are you most thankful for in your personal life, and why?

4. Who are you most thankful for in your professional life, and why?

5. How can you celebrate these individuals this week?

> Competition whose motive is merely to compete, to drive some other fellow out, never carries very far. The competitor to be feared is one who never bothers about you at all, but goes on making his own business better all the time.
>
> —**Henry Ford**

CHAPTER 2

Celebrating as a Catalyst for Change

In society, it is difficult to avoid competition. We are placed in competitive environments within our family, at work, and in school activities. How we view and react to competition elicits a variety of emotions from excitement and exhilaration to fear, frustration, and anxiety. Some individuals are adrenaline junkies who thrive on competing against others or pushing themselves to another level of performance—a personal best. Others, when possible, avoid competition, possibly because of past failures and unwanted feelings of anger and disappointment. Regardless of your perception of competition, the act of competing is prevalent in our society, and it is often used to measure success personally and professionally.

At an early age, competition is minimized. Is the ritual of "everyone gets a trophy" symbolic of recognizing that the individual talents each person brings to the team are important, or is it simply a means to delay the inevitable realization that results matter? Somewhere between third grade and middle school, most of us begin to understand the significance of results. We begin to realize our results determine if we make an athletic team, become a member of a performing arts ensemble, or receive academic recognition. By high school, we acknowledge, for good or bad, that our postsecondary opportunities rely heavily on results.

How did we go from "everyone gets a trophy" to "you're fired" for a lack of results? At this moment, a raging philosophical conversation may be going on in your head. Many of you have already yelled out loud about why we should not be giving every child a trophy and how that small gesture has created a generational perception of entitlement and lack of work ethic. Others are adamantly decrying the detrimental effects stress has on children and adults as a result of the unnecessary pressure to achieve certain results. Regardless of your philosophical stance in this area, as educators, we are in the arena of results, and how we personally adapt and relate plays a significant role in our ability to create winning results for ourselves and for our students to be successful in a results-driven society.

Ensuring Emotionally Healthy Competition

Since competition is virtually impossible to avoid, especially with children and adolescents, we are tasked as educators to pursue a means of competition that is emotionally healthy. For that reason, it is imperative we leverage competition, winning, and celebration to create an environment that allows for productive struggle for students and adults. Research provides a clue to the link between competition and winning. Whether it's the exhilaration of screaming "Bingo!," having the winning number at a raffle, or winning a board game with our family, winning provides our brain with certain feelings not obtained through other means. There is well-documented research relating the positive effects of winning and results to humans. In *The Winner Effect: How Success Affects Brain Chemistry*, Eugene Sheely (2014) finds that "winning will change your biology, making you more likely to overcome increasingly harder challenges in the future." In *The Winner Effect: The Neuroscience of Success and Failure*, Ian H. Robertson (2012) explores the "winner effect," a term he uses to describe how animals increase the release of testosterone and dopamine to the brain after a winning experience. Robertson states the winner effect phenomenon is just as instrumental in humans as it is in other species. Our achievements serve as a catalyst for triggering the brain to expect success. Learning to win and experiencing positive results changes our physiology, creating more resilience and confidence and allowing us to overcome increasingly more difficult obstacles in the future.

Often, winning is symbolized extrinsically; however, the positive impact on long-term success is an intrinsic phenomenon. This has been displayed countless times throughout history. Studying the greatest minds and influencers of our world reveals not a need for celebrity status but, instead, a desire to fundamentally change lives and improve society. It's the passion to become better that leads to the desire to improve current circumstances. Developed confidence in winning through experiences of productive struggle transcends the setbacks of failure and allows the pursuit of success and the realization of a better way to lead, educate, and compete to improve those around us. As educational leaders, we should intentionally promote winning by creating experiences and providing support for staff and students to experience productive struggle. Unfortunately, we often create frustration by exposing staff and students to work and expectations without guidance, encouragement, and celebration.

Planning for and Celebrating Productive Struggle

Cassandra Erkens (2014b) relates productive struggle to confusion as part of the natural learning process. She states the following.

> When learners engage in a productive struggle, they must 1) challenge their own preconceived notions, 2) integrate concepts in a manner that makes sense to them,

and 3) create meaning in a manner that supports their personal integration and retention of the new information or skill.

Beginning, relaunching, or refining the PLC process requires a mindset from district and school leaders that failure is for information, not condemnation. When educational leaders ask teachers to engage in the PLC culture shift, they must encourage a curiosity that asks, "Is there a better way for me to learn and for our students to learn?" This curiosity leads to collective inquiry, which leads to incorporating new practices into collaboration and the classroom.

Productive struggle is essential to break through old paradigms. It is often messy and uncomfortable work, which is why educational leaders must be ready to recognize and celebrate when collaborative teams engage in the collective inquiry process that leads to the implementation of new practices—whether it is in the work of the guiding coalition, behaviors of teacher team members, or instructional practices in the classroom. Educational leaders should rejoice when they observe teachers struggle but continue to try to remove barriers that are preventing team members from learning from each other and barriers preventing all students from learning at high levels. As school leaders, it is imperative to relate Erkens's (2014b) criteria of productive struggle to the work of teachers in a PLC. We must intentionally and with support engage teams in a productive struggle to challenge their own preconceived notions of what it means for learning to be their fundamental purpose, to integrate research-based instructional practices in a manner that makes sense to them, and to create meaning in the PLC culture that supports their personal integration and retention of new practices and procedures. We must encourage teachers to begin "acting their way into a new way of thinking."

Use figure 2.1 (page 36) to anticipate the most predictable areas in the PLC process where collaborative teams tend to struggle. Using this tool allows you to identify and encourage collaborative teams to engage in the struggle and prepares you to support and celebrate the teams that begin acting their way into a new way of thinking.

When planning for productive struggles, it is important to acknowledge the contradiction between the work occurring in a PLC and the traditional approach to competition, winning, and celebration. The traditional approach to competition creates winners and losers with only the winner being celebrated and the losers consoled. A PLC signifies adult professionals learning with and from each other in a community of more than one. In the traditional landscape, competition and winning seem counterintuitive to adult professionals learning with and from each other in a community. However, when the two dynamics form a mutualistic symbiotic relationship, the focus on competition, winning, and celebrations serve to enhance the work of collaborative teams and drive the PLC culture shift.

In our work with one school leadership team relaunching its PLC, we found team members were very concerned with several barriers that prevented past success in the PLC process. One barrier was a shift in the work of teachers collaborating explicitly on issues, questions, and instructional practices that most impact student achievement through the lens of "our students." It became evident during their discussions that the leadership team felt few collaborative teams previously embraced this critical step to ensure all students were positively impacted by every teacher on the team. With this information, the professional development for the entire staff focused on the research and practices connected to student achievement when a team of teachers work interdependently and take collective responsibility for all students learning on or above grade level.

CELEBRATING PRODUCTIVE STRUGGLE TOOL

Directions: Discuss with your instructional leadership team or guiding coalition which collaborative teams may struggle and how your district or school will support and celebrate them through the PLC culture shift.

A Shift in Fundamental Purpose

Expected struggle: Expecting all students to learn and demonstrate proficiency on or above grade level

Which collaborative teams may struggle in this area?

Why do we expect this collaborative team to struggle in this area?

What support is needed for this team to be successful?

How will we monitor progress?

How will we celebrate progress?

A Shift in Use of Assessments

Expected struggle: Developing frequent collaborative team-developed common formative assessments while monitoring each student's proficiency in every essential skill

Which collaborative teams may struggle in this area?

Why do we expect this collaborative team to struggle in this area?

What support is needed for this team to be successful?

How will we monitor progress?

How will we celebrate progress?

A Shift in the Response When Students Don't Learn

Expected struggle: Providing a systematic response that ensures support for every student with multiple opportunities to demonstrate learning

Which collaborative teams may struggle in this area?

Why do we expect this collaborative team to struggle in this area?

What support is needed for this team to be successful?

How will we monitor progress?

How will we celebrate progress?

A Shift in the Work of Teachers

Expected struggle: Collaborating explicitly on issues, questions, and instructional practices that most impact student achievement through the lens of "our students"

Which collaborative teams may struggle in this area?

Why do we expect this collaborative team to struggle in this area?

Figure 2.1: Celebrating productive struggle tool.

continued →

What support is needed for this team to be successful?
How will we monitor progress?
How will we celebrate progress?
A Shift in Focus
Expected struggle: A focus on outputs and results to drive instruction
Which collaborative teams may struggle in this area?
Why do we expect this collaborative team to struggle in this area?
What support is needed for this team to be successful?
How will we monitor progress?
How will we celebrate progress?
A Shift in School Culture
Expected struggle: Planning for short-term wins with frequent specific recognition and a culture of celebration that creates many winners
Which collaborative teams may struggle in this area?

Why do we expect this collaborative team to struggle in this area?

What support is needed for this team to be successful?

How will we monitor progress?

How will we celebrate progress?

A Shift in Professional Development

Expected struggle: Participating in job-embedded learning by collectively working together to assess the impact based on evidence of improved student proficiency

Which collaborative teams may struggle in this area?

Why do we expect this collaborative team to struggle in this area?

What support is needed for this team to be successful?

How will we monitor progress?

How will we celebrate progress?

*Visit **go.SolutionTree.com/PLCbooks** for a free reproducible version of this figure.*

The leadership team ensured every teacher knew why this was a tight, or non-negotiable, foundation of the PLC process and monitored these practices by participating in the collaborative meetings. It took some time and struggle for many teams to relinquish their independent styles and "my students" approach; however, by the end of the school year, every collaborative team reported an increase in collective teacher efficacy and a sense of belonging to their team. To celebrate these practices, teachers were encouraged to share at the end of collaboration how another teacher on their team made them a better instructional leader. By incorporating this celebration practice into their collaboration routine, it became a recurring agenda item, creating an emphasis on sharing the instructional practices that resulted in higher student achievement on both formative and end-of-unit assessments. The strength and efficacy of the team grew each week as team members openly validated a teammate's contribution to their learning and improvement.

Using figure 2.2 allows you to incorporate this celebration into your collaboration or staff meetings to validate and celebrate teammates or staff in one of the foundational pieces of the PLC process—making each other better through the sharing of practices that resulted in more students being proficient or above on the essential learning.

CELEBRATING MY TEAMMATE TOOL

Directions: An essential part of collaboration is discussing what instructional practices led to higher student achievement. Use this tool at the beginning or end of collaboration to celebrate how one of your teammates made you a better instructional leader. Document the procedure, practice, or protocol that you learned from a member of your collaborative team, school leadership team, or district office support team. Part one is for your collaborative team to keep as a reminder of how you are working together to become better in your work. Part two is to share as validation with the person who made you better.

Part One

Name:	Date:	Teammate:
Evidence of Improvement:	**Change in procedure, practice, or protocol from:**	**Change in procedure, practice, or protocol to:**

Part Two		
Name:	Date:	Teammate:
Evidence of Improvement:	Change in procedure, practice, or protocol from:	Change in procedure, practice, or protocol to:

Figure 2.2: Celebrating my teammate tool.

*Visit **go.SolutionTree.com/PLCbooks** for a free reproducible version of this figure.*

Celebrating Teammates

The acknowledgment of hearing and seeing how one teacher impacts their teammates and the students beyond their classroom validates the work of the teacher and the mentality of doing what is necessary for "our team" to get better and for "our students" to perform at higher levels. This celebration provides the necessary information from data to improve collective efficacy and serves as a stimulus for the culture shift from *my students* to *our students* as teachers begin to see how their influence impacts all students through the work of all the teachers on the collaborative team.

The Celebrating My Teammate tool helped one seventh-grade mathematics team create a new paradigm around student investment in their learning. One of the collaborative team's teachers decided her students could not take the end-of-unit assessment until they had demonstrated adequate proof of practice on the formative assessments. The proof of practice required students to complete their formative assessments with a proficient or above score on each learning target before they could take the end-of-unit assessment. Her teammates were skeptical about her new assessment procedure as they were not convinced students would care if they could test on the assigned date. When the end-of-unit assessment date arrived, eight of her thirty mathematics students were instructed to follow the co-teacher to the media center to continue working on their essential mathematics skills for this unit, and when they demonstrated appropriate proof of practice on their formative assessments, they could take the end-of-unit assessment. To the surprise of the teammates, the students were upset they were asked to leave the classroom because they had not demonstrated that they were ready to be successful on the end-of-unit assessment. In the beginning of this new procedure, three of the eight students continued to delay completing their proof of practice; however, within a few weeks, all students in this mathematics classroom conformed to the new assessment criteria, and this mathematics teacher had more students completing their formative assessments, or proof of practice.

Recognizing and celebrating her Tier 1 proficiency improvement, her teammates began using the same procedure for their seventh-grade mathematics students. Within three months, the collaborative team saw a significant improvement in student investment in their learning, a higher percentage of students completing formative assessments, and an increase in the number of students scoring proficient or above on their end-of-unit assessments.

The significance of sharing procedures, practices, or protocols that impact and improve all students learning at higher levels cannot be overstated. Using the Celebrating My Teammate tool (figure 2.2, page 40) validates a teammate's courage to implement a new procedure, creates collective teacher efficacy within the team due to the information from the data showing higher student investment, and improves Tier 1 proficiency. It also gives the school and district administrators an example to showcase and celebrate how looking at data from a common assessment and discussing what occurred in the classroom to get those results created a new approach for the team and a new procedure for other collaborative teams to consider. As a result of this one seventh-grade mathematics teacher acting her way into a new way of thinking, she not only positively impacted her collaborative team, but the proof of practice procedure is now a common K–12 assessment procedure throughout the school district.

Celebrating Layers of Your PLC

If celebrations are the catalyst for change in the PLC process, expectations for competition and winning must change at the school and district levels. If the district is leading the work within the PLC, each school in the district works as a collaborative team to support the district goals and to create the shared knowledge and support required for each school's staff and each collaborative team of teachers to serve and support each other in the PLC process. If the district does not take the lead in creating a guiding coalition or the professional development and support for all schools, each school that embraces the PLC culture shift becomes the PLC, and each collaborative team becomes part of the school's PLC. It is important to realize you are only part of one PLC and that you understand the layers within a PLC in a district and school. As a member of a PLC, you are focused on learning, collaboration, building shared knowledge, helping your teammates get better by sharing practices, being interdependent on each other, and the commitment to *our students* demonstrating proficiency (DuFour et al., 2024). We encourage districtwide PLCs; however, there are many schools, absent of the district's involvement, who create the structure and focus of a PLC and who realize the exceptional results through instructional improvements allowing all students to achieve at higher levels.

Within the PLC, educational leaders must focus on the internal, not external, competition to drive the need to get better for others and not one's self. To do this, wins and celebrations must be established supporting what each team collectively accomplishes and what the sum of all collaborative teams accomplish.

The local school emphasizes grade-level goals, which support school-level goals. For example, Clear Creek Elementary School has a SMART goal to improve students' reading on grade level by 5 percent. To create the PLC mentality, each collaborative team creates a SMART goal of increasing their students' literacy by 5 percent from the previous year. Winning and celebration shifts from isolated teachers who achieved the 5 percent increase for their students to the collaborative teams who collectively achieved the 5 percent increase in student literacy. The competition becomes internal (to get better for my teammates) rather than external (to be individually celebrated). The winning moments and celebrations now occur collectively with teammates—both within the collaborative team and collectively with every collaborative team in the school contributing to the school's SMART goal win.

At the district level, the same approach is taken to create the mentality that the team is the school district and each school is a member of the team. The Bartow County School System begins every school year with a "film study." This school district's film study mirrors athletic teams who review practice and game film to acknowledge success and critique areas for improvement. Instead of film to review past performance, the district studies high-stakes test and data points to acknowledge and celebrate meeting district SMART goals, setting new SMART goals, and studying areas that need improvement.

By engaging in this work as a school district, at each level, elementary, middle, and high schools establish their collective SMART goals, and all levels collectively create a literacy SMART goal. Once the SMART goals are established, each school determines their required levels of improvement to meet the district SMART goals. At the end of each school year, celebrations focus on the success of meeting the district goals. This emphasis drives the internal competition to make each school better.

The internal competition mindset was critical for Bartow County high schools to accomplish their district SMART goal related to improving the graduation rate. In 2018, the Bartow County graduation rate was 87.06 percent. After the district film study, the three high school principals collectively created the district's 2019 graduation SMART goal: at least 90 percent of all 2019 Bartow County School System seniors will graduate in their four-year cohort. With 87.06 percent graduation rate being the ceiling for the school system's graduation, some argued it was more of a stretch SMART goal. However, because this was a collective high school goal, the principals created their own team and met weekly to share data and practices and to monitor the seniors who were on course to graduate. For the first time, in 2019 two Bartow County high schools achieved a graduation rate of over 90 percent; however, the district graduation rate was 89.19 percent—just below the SMART goal. Realizing it was now possible to achieve a 90 percent or above graduation rate at the high school level, the team of high school principals and their school leaders created the 2020 district graduation SMART goal: at least 91 percent of all 2020 Bartow County School System seniors will graduate in their four-year cohort.

With continued collaboration and competition to collectively do what had never been done before in Bartow County, the three high schools combined for a 2020 graduation rate of 91.16 percent. This milestone was a true community win and celebration with news coverage and school board recognition. It was also a celebration to recognize what many thought impossible was now a reality. In 2023, the Bartow County high school graduation rate continued to climb to a new record high of 95.1 percent of seniors graduating in their four-year cohort, and those same principals continue to support each other and compete internally to ensure their school system graduation rate continues to improve every year, resulting in more wins and celebrations for students and staff.

Celebrating Collective Inquiry

The importance of collective inquiry in a PLC has been stated many times. For some educational leaders, the collective inquiry comes from a desire to know if someone else has developed a policy, practice, or procedure that yields better results for student learning. Is there someone getting better results, and if so, how? In the world of educational leadership, any collective inquiry into student achievement leads to Adlai E. Stevenson High School District 125. What was a struggling school and district in the 1980s is now consistently ranked as one of America's best high schools and school districts in the country. Adlai E. Stevenson High School is one of the only high schools in the country to be recognized by the U.S. Department of Education's National Blue Ribbon Schools award five times. In addition, Stevenson has been named a National School of Distinction in Arts Education by the John F. Kennedy Center for the Performing Arts, is the first comprehensive high school designated a New American High School as a model of successful school reform, and is currently ranked as the best school in America by *Niche*. These are uncommon results for any school and school district but especially for a school and district that were once considered undesirable.

Let's use Gary Hoover's (2020) criteria for great businesses to justify our collective inquiry into Adlai E. Stevenson High School District 125 as an example of educational best practices leading to high student achievement. According to Hoover, companies that have the greatest impact on society do so "through innovation, impact on business practices at other companies, and the number of people it affects." First, let's consider the current innovative aspects of education. As principal and superintendent from 1983 to 2002, Richard DuFour was one of the most innovative educational leaders seeking to improve schools through the PLC process, a legacy that continues at Stevenson to this day. The innovative approach removed teachers from teaching in isolation and instead brought teams of teachers together to analyze and improve their classroom practice. DuFour initiated a culture shift in education that established learning as the fundamental purpose of schools and, in turn, shifted the focus from teaching to learning, from what was taught to what was learned, from exposure to content to demonstrated proficiency, and from the teaching of all standards to the guarantee of essential standards and skills. The culture shift occurred at Stevenson High School in the late twentieth century, and the process that is a PLC is still being perfected today with stellar results.

Now let's consider the impact on practices at other organizations as a result of DuFour and his colleagues at Stevenson High School. Today, Stevenson High School is one of the most visited high schools in America. Why do educators from all over the world spend a day or two observing the instructional framework and practices at a single school? Simply, it is the desire in us to understand what makes another organization better. This mentality seeks to bring that same winning, recognition, and celebration to other organizations. It's a curiosity into what policies, practices, and protocols create success for all students. It's our innate focus as educators to create personal best performances for ourselves and our colleagues, and to provide more opportunities for our students to learn how to win. Through the continued success at Adlai E. Stevenson High School and other Model PLC schools, we see best practices delivering consistent uncommon results in relation to where our schools have been and where our schools will consistently stay when operating within a PLC. By 2024, almost four hundred schools and thirty school districts across the world have embraced the PLC culture shift and have adopted the best practices demonstrated at Stevenson High School to be recognized and celebrated as Model PLCs based on the uncommon results where all students have a guaranteed and viable curriculum and where all students are learning at high levels (AllThingsPLC.info, 2024; Cottingham, Hough, & Myung, 2023; Hanson et al., 2021; Solution Tree, 2024j).

Finally, the number of people affected by the PLC at Work process reaches into the millions. Not only are the visitors to Stevenson High School affected by the ongoing work that happens there, but millions of educators have been impacted through PLC at Work schools, conferences, and the knowledge gained from the collective authors of many PLC resources.

As our educational landscape continues to change due to society's expectations, business expectations, and our own understanding of better practices to ensure learning for all students, more and more educational leaders are seeking to acquire the exceptional results seen in PLC schools. The historical significance of Richard DuFour, the many leaders at Stevenson High School, and so many others is still being written, but there is already enough evidence to place them all on the list of people and organizations worthy of our collective inquiry.

How would you rate your natural curiosity to see if there is a better way to improve your leadership skills, classroom instructional practices, or student achievement? When was the last time you were part of a collective inquiry process to see if there is a better way to improve learning for all students? Collective inquiry is essential to compete at higher levels, provide winning moments for staff and students, and fuel more opportunities for celebrations. Figure 2.3 allows you and others in your school or district to engage in the collective inquiry process within each of the PLC's three big ideas: a focus on learning, collaboration and collective responsibility, and results orientation. It also provides an opportunity to celebrate when a specific procedure, practice, or protocol improves because of the collective inquiry process. Use this tool to start, monitor, and celebrate success as a result of collective inquiry.

COLLECTIVE INQUIRY CELEBRATIONS	
Directions: PLCs empower educators to work collaboratively in recurring cycles of collective inquiry. The focus of collective inquiry is to build shared knowledge by utilizing new teaching practices and examining the impact of those results on learning. Use this tool to reflect on the progress your collaborative team is making in collective inquiry and list the celebrations of your change in practice as you are acting your way into a new way of thinking.	
Name of Collaborative Team:	**Your Name (optional):**
Focus on Learning	
Our team has researched national, state, or district curriculum maps to determine what is the most essential learning for our students.	
Our team has researched and come to consensus on how many essential learning standards will comprise our guaranteed and viable curriculum.	
Our team has researched the types of common formative assessments to use for proficiency of student learning.	

Source: Many, Maffoni, Sparks, & Thomas, 2020.
Figure 2.3: Celebrating through collective inquiry tool.

continued →

Our team has researched the rigor required to ensure proficiency on the end-of-unit assessments.

Our team has researched the pedagogical practices that work best in scaffolding the essential learning content.

Our team has researched the most accurate grading process for determining proficiency on the common formative and end-of-unit assessments.

Our team has researched the most logical response to intervention for students during Tier 1 instruction and Tier 2 intervention.

Celebrations:

Collaboration and Collective Commitments

Our team has researched norms to drive our collaboration.

Our team has researched agenda templates to guide our collaboration.

Our team has researched collective commitments to hold ourselves accountable to each other.

Our team has researched data protocols to keep us focused during collaboration.

Our team has researched protocols for sharing the instructional practices that resulted in the information from student assessment data.

Our team has researched highly successful teams from our school or other schools to learn what best practices are used to improve collaboration and student learning.

Celebrations:

Results Orientation

Our team has researched how to use information from student data to determine the success of our teaching practices.

Our team has researched how often we are expected to share common assessment results.

Our team has researched what results we are expected to share.

Our team has researched the format in which we are expected to share student results.

Our team has researched what information we are expected to share in addition to data (intervention plans, extension activities, instructional strategies, and reflection on instructional effectiveness).

Celebrations:

Collective inquiry is necessary for growth within the PLC culture; however, it's the willingness to act on the information that drives the learning. Without action, there are no results to measure the improvement that drives collective teacher efficacy and responsibility. Collective teacher efficacy and responsibility are as much about seeing results as ownership is in the direction. As an educational leader, how do you foster a culture of action without fear of failure? How do you react to teachers and other staff members who tried a new practice but did not get better results?

Embracing Failure

Using celebrations as the catalyst for change within a PLC requires instructional leaders to embrace inquiry failure differently from static failure. *Static failure* is a result of doing the same thing over and over and expecting different results. *Inquiry failure* results from research into best practices and applying those practices to see if you get improved results. In some cases, those practices do not yield improved results, and the experimentation was a result of inquiry failure. What is your leadership tolerance for static failure and inquiry failure?

Growing up an avid Atlanta Braves baseball fan, I (David) rarely missed a game. I was the fan who spent more than three hours every night watching every pitch and the postgame interviews. Embarrassingly, as a grown man, there were nights I did not sleep well because the Braves lost. Those nights were usually due to a late-inning collapse or a thrilling ending where the Braves almost won the game. However, it was one of those nights when I learned the important leadership lesson that failure is for information, not condemnation.

That August night, the Atlanta Braves lost with the tying runner being thrown out at home plate to end the game. It was a relatively close play, but not close enough for the third-base coach to escape criticism for sending the runner home. At that moment, the third-base coach has the authority to hold the runner at third base or send him home. His decision to send him home resulted in the runner being thrown out and the Braves losing the game. Mad, irritated, and extremely frustrated, I waited for Braves manager Bobby Cox's postgame press conference. I watched for only one reason: I wanted to hear him talk about the third-base coach's poor decision to send the runner home that lost the game.

As expected, the first reporter's question centered on the final play of the game. "Bobby, could you take us through the final play of the game and your thoughts on the third-base coach sending the runner home? Are you upset that the runner was sent home, and did you say anything to your coach after the game?"

I knew I would feel much better about the loss when the manager expressed this same irritation and frustration at the third-base coach. Instead, I got a life lesson in leadership that has served me well in my leadership roles. Instead of responding to the loss or failure with condemnation, Bobby Cox celebrated the third-base coach's decision to send the runner home. He shared that good third-base coaches get runners thrown out at home. If runners never get thrown out at home, then the third-base coach isn't being aggressive enough. The runner could have been safe because of a poor throw or the catcher dropping the ball. Cox shared that if the third-base coach had not sent the runner home, he would have been angry.

Speechless, I sat and stared at the television. In my leadership, I never celebrated failure. I couldn't remember a single time when I responded to failure with praise. Failure was always a negative. I wondered why anyone at my school would take a risk based on how I responded to failure. I was sure no one would say that I looked at failure as information, not condemnation.

The evolution of leadership in this area serves as a significant catalyst to the PLC process. When you take the risk out of failure and replace it with the security of failure, your leadership becomes one of empowerment and the stimulus of collective teacher efficacy and responsibility. The stress of being punished if something doesn't go well is replaced with excitement to try something new and loyalty for allowing, promoting, and celebrating staff who choose to act their way into a new way of thinking.

Use figure 2.4 to determine your willingness as a leader to accept that failure is for information, not condemnation. Does your current leadership style promote failure as a risk or as a path to innovation? Do you need to make the final decisions, or do you build the required safety nets to promote failure as a means to improvement? When was the last time you supported a collaborative team for being aggressive in their approach to trying to find a better way to promote learning for each other and the students in the classroom?

RISK TOLERANCE SURVEY

Directions: Circle one rating for each row. Then, record steps that you can take to improve your practice in the last column.

Rating Key: 1 = I have no tolerance for risk taking. (Better safe than sorry!) 2 = I have some tolerance for risk taking. (The glass is half full.) 3 = I am very comfortable encouraging others to take risks. (Fortune favors the brave.)

Your Rating			Key Indicator	Next Steps
1	2	3	Individual collaborative teams developing their own norms	
1	2	3	Individual collaborative teams developing their own SMART goals	
1	2	3	Individual collaborative teams developing new grading procedures	
1	2	3	Individual collaborative teams developing their essential skills and standards	
1	2	3	Individual collaborative teams developing their own common formative assessments	
1	2	3	Individual collaborative teams developing their own common end-of-unit assessments	
1	2	3	Individual teachers allowed to try new instructional practices	
1	2	3	The guiding coalition or leadership team being allowed to make the final decision through consensus	

Figure 2.4: Risk tolerance survey.

*Visit **go.SolutionTree.com/PLCbooks** for a free reproducible version of this figure.*

Conclusion

How would you rate yourself, your colleagues, your school, and district leadership in promoting celebrations for staff and students? Do you see a staff just trying to survive, or are you celebrating a staff hungry to compete at a high level by embracing a mentality that if it's being done successfully somewhere, it can be done successfully here? Have you accepted the same norms that have prevented teachers and administrators from ensuring all students are learning on or above grade level, or is the competitor in you ready to change the narrative and celebrate the positive academic success with your students, your school, your school district, and your community? Use the questions (page 50) and journal prompts (page 52) to reflect on the ideas in this chapter from an organizational and then a personal viewpoint.

Uncommon academic results are happening today in many schools and districts that look just like your school and district. Those schools and districts have developed instructional leaders who embrace innovation and positively impact the practices and behaviors of others. They embrace celebrations as a catalyst in the PLC culture to ensure teachers and administrators know the value of focusing on the three big ideas of a PLC: a focus on learning, collaboration and collective responsibility, and results.

Here's the great news for the competitor in you: there are no outliers in the PLC at Work journey. When school leaders embrace collective inquiry and value productive struggle, teachers feel confident in acting their way into a new way of thinking because they know that failure is for information, not condemnation. As we will learn in chapter 3 (page 55), leadership matters in this work. The navigation of internal competition, small wins, and intentional celebrations is significant in leading the PLC culture shift.

Chapter 2 Reflection Questions

Reflect on these questions from an organizational viewpoint.

1. As an educational leader, how do you look at competition? Do you create opportunities for internal competitions?

2. As an educational leader, how do you foster a culture of action without fear of failure?

3. How do you react to teachers and other staff members who tried a new practice but did not get better results?

4. Does your current leadership style promote failure as a risk or as a path to innovation?

5. Do you need to make the final decisions, or do you build the required safety nets to promote failure as a means to improvement?

6. What is your leadership tolerance for static failure compared to inquiry failure?

7. When was the last time you supported a collaborative team for being aggressive in their approach to trying to find a better way to promote learning for each other and the students in the classroom?

8. How can you celebrate someone or a collaborative team this week for showing resilience through productive struggle?

Celebrating in a PLC at Work® © 2025 Solution Tree Press • SolutionTree.com
Visit **go.SolutionTree.com/PLCbooks** to download this free reproducible.

Chapter 2 Journal Prompts

Reflect on these questions from a personal viewpoint.

1. Do you view competition with excitement and exhilaration or with fear, frustration, and anxiety?

2. In competition, are you motivated more by winning or by having a personal best performance?

3. In your leadership role, how can you leverage someone's approach to competition?

4. Have you ever worked for someone who treated failure not for information, but for condemnation? If so, how did it make you feel in your daily work?

5. Have you ever worked for someone who treated failure as information, not condemnation? If so, how did it make you feel in your daily work?

6. When was the last time you had a productive struggle in your professional life? What was the outcome?

7. How would you describe your level of resilience in your professional life? Is it different from your level of resistance in your personal life? If so, why?

Effort and courage are not enough without purpose and direction.

—John F. Kennedy

CHAPTER 3

Leveraging Celebrations in Your Leadership

We all have moments when we hear or see something that forever changes our way of thinking and acting. These are our transformational moments, experiences that have shaped us and given us the wisdom, clarity, purpose, and direction to be successful. In one such experience, a young first-year middle school principal was struggling to believe he could make any difference in his school's poor academic performance. The difficulty of leading a "needs improvement" school with over 90 percent of the students living in poverty weighed heavily on him, and he was quickly falling into an "It can't be done here" mentality. Despite his initial optimism and enthusiasm, his midyear assessment of his leadership provided no better results than to watch teachers and students go through the motions of the school day with no hope or efficacy. As he was beginning to accept his isolated supporting role of getting through each day, he had a chance encounter with another leader who simply said to him, "If someone can do the job better than you, then get out of the way and let them do it. The job is too important to be unsuccessful."

This was a pivotal moment for this young principal—the exact message he needed to hear. His pride alone was enough to prevent him from abdicating his responsibilities to someone else, but it was the last part of the message that caused his insistent quest to get better and to help those around him be more successful. Yes, the job of the principal was too important to be unsuccessful, and if someone could do it better, he should get out of the way and let that person lead. This unexpected encounter caused the principal to begin to examine and better understand how other principals led similar schools to achieve exceptional academic results for students. Further inquiry led to a clear understanding of the importance of building efficacy in others; how collaboration is the key to improving leadership and teaching practices, a necessity for creating hope and efficacy in students; and why student proficiency on essential standards is the measure of success in student achievement. With a transformed leadership approach, the young principal facilitated a school culture shift that led to his middle school being removed from the "needs improvement" list and becoming a Title I School of Distinction.

A glance at the hundreds of Model PLC schools and their stories on the AllThingsPLC website (www.AllThingsPLC.info) provides school leaders with the foundational pieces of success for all students to learn on or above grade level. However, what many overlook or don't see in their stories is the importance for district or school leadership to celebrate the culture shift that epitomizes a PLC. As mentioned in the previous chapters, celebrating staff throughout the process engages those doing the work to build the efficacy required to sustain the challenges of the change process, and celebrating requires monitoring.

This chapter focuses on the district or school leader's fundamental shift in their approach to leadership in the PLC process. There are certain foundations that every school is tight about to achieve the desired academic results. This chapter provides what is tight or non-negotiable in the leadership of a PLC (intentional leadership and leading through a guiding coalition) and provides monitoring tools to celebrate and ensure your leadership is having the desired effect of building efficacy and responsibility throughout the school or district staff.

Intentional Leadership in a PLC

In *Visible Learning,* John Hattie (2009) finds that the school leader has a relatively low effect size (0.33 standard deviations) on student achievement. To put this into perspective, the average school leader has an impact of less than one year of growth on student learning. This revelation is not easy for most district or school leaders to accept, and it certainly defies the impact Richard DuFour had as principal and superintendent of Adlai E. Stevenson High School as described in chapter 2 (page 33), the impact our young middle school principal had on his school, and countless other examples of turnaround schools and the leaders who ushered in their exceptional results. So why does Hattie's research indicate most district and school leaders have little impact on student achievement? Could it be as simple as understanding certain types of leadership behaviors matter more than others?

Tim Waters, Robert J. Marzano, and Brian McNulty (2003) at Mid-Continent Research for Education and Learning (McREL) identify certain behaviors that, when practiced by district and school leaders, are likely to "promote significant improvement in student achievement" (p. 8). As Viviane Robinson states, "The more leaders focus their influence, their learning, and their relationships with teachers on the core business of teaching and learning, the greater their likely influence on student outcomes" (as cited in Robinson, Lloyd, & Rowe, 2008, p. 636). If our fundamental purpose is truly centered on *learning*, shouldn't district and school leadership also be results oriented and measure success on how well all students are learning on or above grade level on what teachers have identified as the most essential learning? Moving leadership from intentions to results orientation requires leaders to examine their influence in relation to learning—the learning of adults and students.

Most district and school leaders do not want to be average, much less below-average, leaders. Both main decision makers of a school district or school, the superintendent and the principal, are coveted positions that few get an opportunity to experience. In most cases, superintendents and principals have been successful teachers and successful assistant principals. They have a history of winning and achieving exceptional results for themselves and others. Each superintendent and principal was selected from among a group of successful principals or assistant principals who desired the chance to lead a district or school and make a positive impact. So, if the "best of the best" are being selected, why are so many districts and schools led by superintendents and principals who make such an insignificant difference in learning? To answer this question, consider the following leadership parable about three principals, a horse, and the first day of school.

Three principals were told that they would each receive a horse on the first day of school. While sitting in his office, the first principal looked out the window and saw his horse. Knowing the horse would arrive, he was anxious and overcome with excitement. He ran frantically out of his office, through the front lobby of the school, and directly toward the horse. The principal had never been on a horse before, but he didn't care as this was his dream. As a boy, he always wanted a horse, and he would finally get to ride one. Not waiting for instructions on how to ride the horse or even for the saddle and reins to be put on the horse, the principal jumped on and began screaming for the horse to run. As the horse obeyed and began sprinting away, the principal was thrown off and watched his horse get smaller and smaller as it ran from him. Though hurt and dejected, the principal could not wait to jump back on the horse, if it ever returned.

Sitting in her office preparing for the traditional opening day of school, the second principal did not see her horse when it arrived in the school parking lot, but she did notice the horse when it was brought into the school lobby. Just as her secretary announced her horse had arrived and seeing it for the first time, the principal suddenly became intrigued by the thought of owning a horse. She cautiously approached the horse and asked for the manual on how to ride a horse. Upon receiving the manual and all the gear necessary to ride and care for the horse, the principal began reading the manual aloud to the horse as if the horse needed to hear the instructions as well. She laid the gear out across the ground and spent time practicing with the gear away from the horse. After reading the manual many times and practicing with the saddle, stirrups, and reins, the principal sought out the advice of other horse owners to get their thoughts on the best way to ride a horse. After many weeks of talking to the horse, talking to others, and talking to herself, the principal still did not feel she knew enough about riding a horse, so she decided to not ride the horse until she could talk to more people about horses.

Finally, sitting in his office, the third principal did not notice when his horse arrived. The horse and all its gear were moved from the school parking lot to the school's front lobby, and then into the principal's office. Even with the smells and noises of the horse, somehow the principal still did not notice his horse had arrived. His secretary, an assistant principal, and the school's teacher of the year all shared with him that he had a horse in his office, but somehow, he didn't comprehend what they were telling him. He just couldn't see the horse, and he wondered why people kept telling him he had a horse in his office. At the end of the day, he was angry that his horse never arrived.

How many instructionally ineffective district or school leaders are closely aligned with one of these three principals? Principal One is acting his way into a new way of thinking, but he does so carelessly and without a plan of action or system in place for success. He doesn't learn from his mistakes, and he doesn't see the need to ask others for advice. Principal Two is trying to think her way into a new way of acting. She researches and talks to anyone and everyone, but she never feels comfortable enough to act. Finally, Principal Three cannot see what everyone else sees. He is unable to notice something has changed in his environment—even when everyone around him can see the change.

In many districts and schools embracing the PLC process, there are teachers and other staff who see the value of focusing on learning, collaborating, and being results oriented; however, they can only get so far before they need assistance to get to the depth of the work necessary for teachers to use data to drive student learning decisions and improve teaching practices to ensure all students are learning on or above grade level. The three principals in our parable would each be equally ineffective in leading the staff in the PLC process but for different reasons.

Principal One is excited about the opportunity to get better through the PLC process. He has heard how many schools have implemented it successfully and the great results the PLC process has produced for staff and students. His "Let's go!" mentality is encouraging, but his lack of understanding that a PLC is a process to perfect and not a program to complete prevents him from successfully leading his staff in the culture shift. Though his attitude of acting his way into a new way of thinking is admirable, his lack of understanding of the PLC process, lack of building shared knowledge with the staff, and lack of creating collective teacher efficacy only causes frustration and logical resistance due to the staff not understanding *why* a change will deliver better results or *how* the changes will work in their current instructional environment.

Principal Two is equally ineffective in her leadership because she is trying to think her way into a new way of acting. She knows her staff and students are not getting the results of all students learning on or above grade level, but she is hesitant to introduce the PLC process to the staff because it might not work at her school. She knows the PLC process is built on best practices, and she knows other schools have implemented the changes with improved academic results for all students, but she is not confident she can successfully be the change agent for a PLC in her school. As a result, she never acts her way into a new way of thinking, and therefore, the status quo for teacher practices and student learning stays the same.

Finally, Principal Three doesn't see any need to change. Although everyone around him is aware the school culture promotes instructional inequity with a lack of a guaranteed and viable curriculum, teachers teaching in isolation, and students being left behind when they did not learn something the first time, he does not see any need for change. Principal Three sees nothing that warrants a change in the status quo.

In too many districts and schools, the superintendent or principal either acts their way into a new way of thinking without building the necessary efficacy and plan of engagement, is paralyzed by thinking their way into a new way of acting or is simply unaware that staff and students could be winning more in their fundamental purpose of learning. Do you have any of these tendencies in your leadership? If so, use figure 3.1 to indicate what represents your "horse," where you need to see change and what needs to happen for you to act with a plan for success, where you need to see improvements in your leadership, and who you need to include to achieve improvements. This reflective exercise is best used when combined with the vulnerability of asking someone who knows you well to read the parable of the three principals, a horse, and the first day of school and complete figure 3.1 as feedback on your leadership. Did you come to the same conclusion? If not, what surprised you from the feedback? If so, how can you use the confirmation to establish a starting point for improving your influence on student achievement?

FEEDBACK ON YOUR LEADERSHIP QUESTIONAIRE
Directions: After reading the parable about three principals, a horse, and the first day of school, answer the following questions.
Do you have any of these tendencies in your leadership?
If so, what represents your horse?
Where do you need to see change, and what needs to happen for you to act with a plan for success?

Figure 3.1: Three principals, a horse, and the first day of school—Feedback on your leadership.

continued →

Where do you need to see exceptional results in your leadership?

Who do you need to include in your journey to achieve these exceptional results?

Visit **go.SolutionTree.com/PLCbooks** *for a free reproducible version of this figure.*

Leading With a Guiding Coalition

Effective district and school leadership in a PLC continually asks the following questions.

1. Are we building collective leader and teacher efficacy in our decision-making process?
2. Is there clarity in why a culture shift is needed for our district or school?
3. Is there clarity in how we are going to move forward to get better results for all students?
4. Do we have a high-functioning team to provide honest feedback, address barriers to learning, and come to consensus on decisions pertaining to issues within the PLC process?

To address these questions, we must agree that we do not support teachers teaching in isolation, and we cannot accept leaders leading in isolation. For that reason, one of the first steps in the PLC journey is the creation of a *guiding coalition* (DuFour et al., 2024), a small group of thoughtful and respected instructional leaders within the school who embrace the opportunity to act their way into a new way of thinking. Beginning with a smaller group enhances the likelihood of building consensus later within the larger group. The guiding coalition is critical at both the district and school levels (DuFour et al., 2024). The superintendent or principal leads the guiding coalition of high-functioning decision makers through subcommittees building shared knowledge about best practice—with *best practice* defined as those practices that have a positive impact on student success. The superintendent or principal encourages experimentation aimed at closing the gaps in student achievement, and the guiding coalition members are actively analyzing, discussing, and reflecting on instructional practices with the intention to discover a better approach to student learning.

According to Richard DuFour, Rebecca DuFour, Robert Eaker, and Thomas W. Many (2010), principals of PLCs must be clear about their primary responsibilities, disperse leadership throughout the school, engage educators in a culture of reciprocal accountability where responsibility is more important that authority, and bring coherence to the complexities of schooling by aligning the structure and culture of the school with its core purpose.

These four responsibilities of the principal also apply to the superintendent and their leadership at the district level. We agree with Bill Hall (2022) that principals must involve identified critical staff members as a guiding coalition to build a solid foundation of the PLC process, develop shared knowledge in the areas of the PLC culture shift, reach consensus on critical changes to ensure learning for all students, and protect the work from being undermined by resistors of change. We contend that superintendents follow the same model and build a district guiding coalition to build the district's shared knowledge, collective leader efficacy, implementation timeline, and avenue to role-model expected behaviors and outcomes in local schools.

This transition in leadership is critical in acting your way into a new way of thinking with a plan and a purpose. It is only through the work of a guiding coalition that leaders create an insurance policy to get through the challenges that come with any change initiative. It also requires principals to move from leading in isolation to leading collaboratively. This is in stark contrast to the autocratic principals from past generations who were expected to make all the difficult decisions with very little support. In fact, many superintendents and principals, past and present, exemplify what Margaret Wheatley and Deborah Frieze (2011) describe as the *hero leader*. The district and school's guiding coalition is the perfect and necessary segue for superintendents and principals to transition from trying to be the hero of the district or school and instead become the *host*.

Wheatley and Frieze (2011) describe in *From Hero to Host* how many leaders assume and often seek the role of *hero*. The leader who will quickly solve the school's problems makes things instantly better for the staff, and provides a sense of expert control to handle difficult situations.

> The only predictable consequence of leaders' attempts to wrest control of a complex, even chaotic situation, is that they create more chaos. They go into isolation with just a few key advisors and attempt to find a simple solution (quickly) to a complex problem. (Wheatley & Frieze, 2011)

Instead, Wheatley and Frieze (2011) advocate for school leaders to transition to the role of *host*, a leader who establishes a culture for collaboration by creating a system where other leaders within the organization have the time to identify and work through complex issues and barriers preventing progress and success. A leader serving as a host creates opportunities to inspire efficacy in those doing the work to solve the complex issues and then to publicly celebrate their achievements. It is imperative leaders in a PLC embody the characteristics of a host and guard against the allurement of being a hero.

The host is engaged in the work with staff instead of someone trying to solve problems for them. In the PLC process, those doing the work are doing the learning; therefore, it is important school and district leaders work side by side with a small team of instructional leaders to engage in problem solving and building shared knowledge. Within this framework of leadership, leaders must establish guidelines to monitor and acknowledge the success of ownership within the team and to self-monitor and celebrate when you build collective efficacy and responsibility instead of being the hero that, "truth be told, they never wanted . . . to rescue them anyway" (Wheatley & Frieze, 2011).

When the leader serves as a host, a philosophical change is evident to everyone in the district or school. The superintendent or principal is no longer the individual instructional leader of the school but instead becomes the leader of the district or school's guiding coalition. The guiding coalition transforms into the instructional leadership of the district or school. Hattie's (2009) research finds that one of the most significant effects on learning is empowering teachers to know they are making a difference in student learning by giving them the power to collectively make instructional decisions and support the evidence collected from assessments. Hattie states the practice of building collective teacher efficacy and responsibility leads to an effect size of 1.57 standard deviations; that is almost four years of academic growth for students, and it has nothing to do with the students directly, but it has everything to do with leadership.

Creating the Guiding Coalition

The true effect size of collective teacher efficacy is only possible when instructional leadership of the district or school transitions from the superintendent or principal to the guiding coalition. Some may see the transition of power as minimizing the role of the superintendent or principal; it is, in fact, the opposite. In most cases, a superintendent or principal trying to individually change the culture of a district or school is like a captain trying to quickly turn around a cruise ship in an Alaskan glacial bay. With all good intentions, it just doesn't happen. However, when a superintendent or principal embodies the host mentality, they now invite a small team of selected representatives of each subject area to become the champions and guardians of the PLC culture shift.

When a guiding coalition of staff members demonstrate positional power, expertise, credibility, and leadership and are led by a superintendent or principal who's focused on developing their PLC knowledge to lead the district or school, you immediately begin to see collective leader and teacher efficacy and a collective responsibility for improvement and success. The superintendent or principal goes from leading in isolation to being the leader of the most influential team on campus, a team charged with leading the PLC journey. The culture shift occurs more quickly because information is disseminated from the macrolevel of the guiding coalition to the microlevel when each guiding coalition member delivers critical information to their collaborative team.

In *Powerful Guiding Coalitions: How to Build and Sustain the Leadership Team in Your PLC at Work*, Bill Hall (2022) outlines the separation of duties between the guiding coalition and the traditional leadership team. Hall states the guiding coalition is responsible for everything involving the PLC process, and the leadership team is responsible for everything else in the building. The reason for the delineation is to ensure the evolution of the professional learning, implementation, and progress monitoring for the PLC doesn't devolve into an operational agenda quagmire. Discipline, student schedules, bus routes, lunch schedules, pep rallies, and assemblies are all important to the functioning of a school; however, none of these issues will result in teachers and students achieving extraordinary results in the academic arena. Since these operational issues are so important, the district or school should have a leadership team focused on ensuring they are executed at a high level. The leadership team should continue to meet regularly with norms and an agenda reflecting their focused work. In turn, the guiding coalition should also meet regularly with norms and an agenda reflecting their focused work around the three big ideas of learning, collaboration, and results.

To ensure collective efficacy and responsibility within the district or school, the superintendent or principal should model and create collective efficacy and responsibility within the school guiding coalition. With a "train the trainer" mentality, the superintendent or principal should expect the guiding coalition members to replicate the PLC information with their collaborative teams. With the school leadership team focused on the operational aspects of the school, the guiding coalition is tasked with coming to consensus, removing identified barriers to the PLC culture shift, and redelivering to the staff every decision made within the PLC journey. For the district or school just beginning the PLC journey, agenda items may include creating a glossary of common PLC terms for clarity and establishing a mission, vision, collective commitments, and goals that indicate learning is the fundamental purpose of the school.

For the district or school restarting the PLC process or into the second year of the journey, agenda items may include how to ensure focused weekly collaborative team meetings based on what students are required to learn and how to best assess their learning, incorporating the four critical questions (see page 20) as the basis for each collaborative team meeting, implementing an essential standards process and identifying essential and supporting standards, establishing SMART goals in each teacher collaborative team, and identifying future PLC professional learning necessary to function at a higher level and deliver the uncommon results in learning, collaboration, and results (Eaker, Hagadone, Keating, & Rhoades, 2021).

Regardless of where you are in your PLC journey, results occur when the guiding coalition has developed collective leader efficacy. Our work has provided frequent examples where districts and schools create, develop, and allow the guiding coalition to lead can see faster and more significant increases in student achievement. For that reason, it is critical to get the right people aligned on the guiding coalition to be the guardians for the PLC culture shift. With school districts, we recommend including each principal serving on the guiding coalition along with the central office academic support staff. In large school districts, it may be beneficial to have separate guiding coalitions for each level: elementary, middle, and high school. It is important for each principal to serve as a participant in the district-guiding coalition to see how it should look at their school and to build the collective efficacy in the shared knowledge and implementation timeline.

Our work with schools has seen principals use one of three approaches to establish a guiding coalition.

1. One approach, the least abrasive and least effective, is to rename the current leadership team the school's guiding coalition. This approach causes the least

turmoil, but ultimately, it slows the work necessary to achieve the uncommon results from the PLC. Rarely do all the school's current leadership team members meet the criteria to be a member of the guiding coalition. Remember, the criteria are centered on staff members who have positional power, expertise, credibility, and leadership in the instructional arena. There are members of each school's leadership team who are highly qualified to be members on both the leadership team and the guiding coalition; however, there are also valuable members of the leadership team who will not bring value to the guiding coalition.

2. The second approach to create the school's guiding coalition is to abolish the current leadership team and announce there will be a new team leading the school (the guiding coalition). The principal shares the why behind the transition from a leadership team to a guiding coalition. During the meeting, the principal can provide staff with an application to apply, or the selection may be by invitation only. The principal and other administrative leaders carefully discuss who will best serve the faculty and students by being a member of the most influential team guiding the school through the PLC journey. While many schools have chosen this path, guard against the work of a leadership team encroaching on the work of the guiding coalition. Too many times, the operational agenda overcomes the instructional PLC agenda. If a school chooses this approach to establishing the guiding coalition, it is recommended to have two separate agendas and a start and finish time to discuss the PLC work and the operational work.

3. Finally, the third approach in creating a school's guiding coalition is to continue with the leadership team and create the guiding coalition as a separate team to focus on the PLC culture shift. As with the second approach, the principal provides clarity to the staff regarding why the school will create a new team (the guiding coalition). They explain how the members will be selected, by application or invitation, and the time commitment and importance of the new team. This approach is recommended for two reasons.

    → The leadership team is critical to the school operating at a high level. As some agenda items will shift to the guiding coalition, it is beneficial for the leadership team to continue its work without interruption.

    → Though some members will overlap between the leadership team and the guiding coalition, there will be new members of the instructional staff included in the guiding coalition and other staff members added to the leadership team. With the addition of new staff to both teams, the school expands the collective leader efficacy within the school. The expansion of collective leader and teacher efficacy always leads to greater achievement.

Selecting Your Guiding Coalition

Once you determine how you will create the guiding coalition, the next step is choosing the members. With such responsibility entrusted with this team, it is necessary to get the right instructional staff to assume the leadership responsibility and embrace the accountability of all students learning on or above grade level. As mentioned, there are two ways to select the inaugural or first-generation guiding coalition team members: by application or invitation. Both selection methods work well; it is personal preference as to which to use, with the critical piece being who to choose, not how. Getting this personnel decision wrong can slow down or eliminate the possibility of a high-functioning PLC focused on learning, collaboration, and results.

One method we recommend for the principal and others tasked with the selection process is using the Hersey-Blanchard Situational Leadership Model (Hersey, Blanchard, & Johnson, 2013) for selecting the first guiding coalition members. This method has proven to be extremely successful both in the selection of members for the guiding coalition and as an excellent reflection tool and leadership exercise for administrators.

The Hersey-Blanchard Situational Leadership Model encourages leaders to evaluate staff into one of four categories.

1. Willing and able
2. Willing but unable
3. Unwilling but able
4. Unwilling and unable

In this model, staff are willing and able if they have the passion and skill set to perform the task. These are staff members who have a great attitude for the right work and who have demonstrated the skills necessary to get results. These are the individuals to whom you delegate responsibility, whose efforts you support, and who you let be successful.

Staff who are willing but unable have the passion and a great attitude for the right work, but currently do not possess the skills to garner the desired results. With a passion for collective inquiry and collaboration, these staff members need coaching to improve their skill set and become members of the willing and able group.

The third group is the unwilling but able staff members. These individuals have the skill set and have been successful in the past but currently lack the passion or positive attitude to impact others. With these individuals, a supporting humanistic leadership approach is needed to change their passion and help them become members of the willing and able group.

Finally, the unwilling and unable staff members do not have the passion and positive attitude or the skill set for the right work. These individuals are a hindrance and a burden on the entire staff working toward positive culture changes. As a leader, you must direct and micromanage their work. There are few success stories of unwilling and unable personnel bringing value to their current organization. For this reason and after an effort to move the unwilling and unable into another category, the work must be done to give this employee a fresh start somewhere else.

In a PLC, teacher teams know their students are learning by target and by standard. PLCs often have student "data walls" where staff can see posted data for how each student is doing academically and the progress they are making throughout the year. For leaders, using the Hersey-Blanchard Situational Leadership Model is similar to a student data wall. Instead of students listed by name under the learning categories of beginning learner, developing learner, proficient learner, and distinguished learner, the school leader lists each staff member by name under the categories of willing and able, willing but unable, unwilling but able, and unwilling and unable. As Hattie's (2009) research indicates, teachers improve student learning by visually knowing where each student is in their learning progressions. We believe that leaders will lead better when they know where each person is in the organization from a willing and able standpoint. By visually listing each staff member in one of the four categories, leaders now have groups of staff to intentionally lead and improve through delegating, coaching, supporting, or directing.

The principal and a small team of evaluators can use the worksheet in figure 3.2 or a similar tool to identify those staff members who are currently willing and able from an instructional leadership and building leadership capacity. In *Leading With Intention*, Jeanne Spiller and Karen Power (2019) provide a tool for selecting and reflecting on guiding coalition members as another example of a tool used to reflect on who to include in a guiding coalition. Through these exercises, leaders identify those staff members who need to be on the guiding coalition, those staff members who will be your second-generation guiding coalition members, and those staff members who will predictably be doubters who will need to be convinced of the value of the team and resisters to remove.

GUIDING COALITION MEMBER SELECTION WORKSHEET							
Directions: Using the Hersey-Blanchard Situational Leadership Model, rate each instructional staff member as willing and able, willing but unable, unwilling but able, or unwilling and unable.							
Rating Key: 1 = Willing and able; 2 = Willing but unable; 3 = Unwilling but able; 4 = Unwilling and unable							
Your Rating				Name of Instructional Staff Member	Guiding Coalition Member		
					Yes	Maybe	No
1	2	3	4				
1	2	3	4				
1	2	3	4				
1	2	3	4				
1	2	3	4				
1	2	3	4				
1	2	3	4				

Figure 3.2: Guiding coalition member selection worksheet.

*Visit **go.SolutionTree.com/PLCbooks** for a free reproducible version of this figure.*

Staff members who are identified as willing and able in instructional leadership and building leadership must be on your guiding coalition. We define *instructional leadership* as any academic or behavioral instructional staff member who understands the need for interdependency with teammates, embraces collective inquiry to improve instructional practices, and seeks opportunities to learn and share best practices with teammates. We define *building leadership* as any academic or behavioral instructional staff member who embraces change as an opportunity to improve practices; understands the need to reach consensus before initiating new policies, practices, or protocols; and has the fortitude to address staff who may be resistant to any change in the school culture. Spiller and Power (2019) suggest looking at staff members to complete the guiding coalition who characterize positional power, expertise, credibility, and leadership since principals must be able to delegate the work to build collective efficacy and begin PLC work with staff who have the passion and skill set to embrace the necessary professional learning while influencing their peers to see the value in the PLC culture shift.

Figure 3.3, presenting the responsibilities and actions of a guiding coalition, combines the individual responsibilities and the corresponding actions expected from each guiding coalition member. Clarity about expectations for each member and team responsibilities ensures the most qualified staff participate in the guiding coalition. We encourage leaders to use figure 3.3 when explaining to staff the purpose of the guiding coalition and as a point of discussion during the first guiding coalition meeting. It will help you as the guiding coalition leader to know where individual members see themselves as having strengths in these areas and which of the responsibilities and actions give them anxiety. Not all members will have strengths in all areas. This is an opportune time to remind the guiding coalition members about the importance of being interdependent as the collective team needs the strengths of each member to successfully fulfill the responsibilities of the guiding coalition. It also is an opportunity to celebrate the diverse talents of your team and why that diversity is critical in working with all staff to have the same clarity throughout the PLC journey.

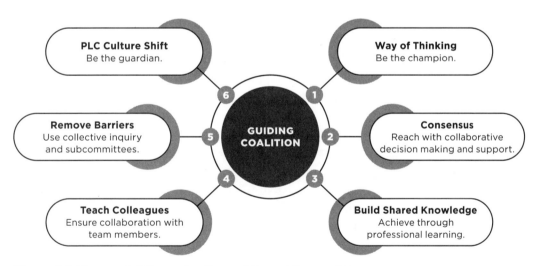

Figure 3.3: Responsibilities and actions of the guiding coalition.

*Visit **go.SolutionTree.com/PLCbooks** for a free reproducible version of this figure.*

In our experience, there are occasions where a principal does not have enough willing and able members of the instructional staff. Since the school's guiding coalition should be representative of each subject or grade level, principals must choose between having a smaller guiding coalition that does not represent all instructional areas of the school and including staff members who are not willing and able. In this situation, carefully consider adding staff from the willing but unable category. We have found willing but unable staff members are typically more successful members of the guiding coalition than the unwilling but able staff members. The professional learning that occurs in guiding coalition meetings will move these staff members to willing and able status. Principals who have chosen an unwilling but able staff member for the guiding coalition have often been forced to remove the individual during or after the first year due to negativity or resistance.

Empowering the Guiding Coalition

Once the school's guiding coalition is established, it begins meeting regularly with established norms, commitments, goals, and agenda items connected to the PLC culture shift: developing collective responsibility for student learning, selecting a guaranteed and viable curriculum, using common formative assessments to monitor student learning, using common assessments to determine the most successful teaching practices, and creating a systematic intervention and extension schedule. Their focus is to become experts in the work of a PLC and drive the schoolwide professional learning toward a culture shift focused on the school's fundamental purpose of learning for all students.

To increase collective leader efficacy beyond the guiding coalition, the guiding coalition creates subcommittees in response to each barrier. These subcommittees, comprised of guiding coalition members and other recruited instructional staff, use collective inquiry to identify solutions to overcoming a particular barrier and makes recommendations to the guiding coalition on what steps to take. Once the guiding coalition reaches consensus on steps to take, the subcommittee presents to the staff the necessary changes so the school can move forward in the PLC journey.

Figure 3.4 is a subcommittee tool showing a list of potential barriers many schools and districts face in their PLC transformation. Use this tool to identify subcommittees, identify members, monitor their progress, and celebrate their successes.

SUBCOMMITTEE PARTICIPANT TABLE						
Subcommittee	Elementary	Middle School	High School	Central Office	Progress Monitoring *Date to Present*	Celebration *Date of Change*
Assessment and Data						
Discipline and Positive Behavioral Interventions and Supports (PBIS)						
Essential Standards						

Glossary of Key PLC Terms						
Grading						
Monitoring PLC Processes						
Response to Intervention						
Scheduling Collaboration						
Templates						
Training						

Figure 3.4: Subcommittee participant table.

*Visit **go.SolutionTree.com/PLCbooks** for a free reproducible version of this figure.*

In the teaching-assessing cycle, collaborative teams of teachers build summative assessments before beginning Tier 1 instruction. This backward-design model ensures students receive instruction on every learning target the assessment assesses. We recommend using figure 3.5 (page 70), the "guiding coalition leadership efficacy analysis" tool developed by Bartow County School System, as a backward design summative assessment of your guiding coalition.

This tool provides insight into the work of the guiding coalition. At the end of each school year, guiding coalition members anonymously complete the tool to provide feedback for the principal. The principal uses the results to monitor how well they are creating collective leader efficacy within the guiding coalition. The guiding coalition members use the results to monitor next steps for the principal's leadership and their work to ensure the indicators become embedded in the school culture. Upon completion of the analysis, we recommend you utilize figure 3.6 (page 72), also developed by the Bartow County School System. This tool walks the guiding coalition through steps to celebrate strengths and uncover weaknesses of the guiding coalition based on the results of the analysis and a section to develop an action plan blueprint to address areas of need and monitor progress and celebrate success.

			GUIDING COALITION LEADERSHIP EFFICACY ANALYSIS TOOL	
	**Directions:** Circle one rating for each row. If your score is below a 3, record your next steps to improve your rating.	
	**Rating key:** 1 = Not evident; 2 = Compliant (meeting the minimum requirements); 3 = Embedded in our culture. L = Leadership, FL = Focus on learning, C = Collaboration, RO = Results orientation.	
colspan=3	Rating	Key Indicator	Next Steps
1	2	3	**L1. Building Collaborative Teacher Efficacy**	
			There is a shared belief by our guiding coalition members that we have the skills and empowerment to positively impact collaborative teams.	
1	2	3	**L2. Supporting the PLC Culture**	
			Our guiding coalition is the catalyst for the PLC process. We have a mission, a vision, and collective commitments that drive our work.	
1	2	3	**L3. All Members of the Guiding Coalition Are Willing and Able**	
			The members of our guiding coalition have a passion for the PLC work and the skill set to implement the right work.	
1	2	3	**L4. The Guiding Coalition Holds Accountable Resistors and Doubters**	
			There is a process in place for members of the guiding coalition to address and hold accountable staff members who are resistors or doubters of the PLC process.	
1	2	3	**L5. Clarity of Loose and Tight PLC Expectations**	
			The members of the guiding coalition know the tight PLC characteristics and understand how to use the loose characteristics to build collective teacher efficacy.	
1	2	3	**L6. Monitoring the PLC Process**	
			The guiding coalition fosters a culture that has a clear monitoring plan to determine which collaborative teams are functioning at a high level and which collaborative teams need assistance in learning, collaboration, and results.	
1	2	3	**L7. Celebrating the Right Work**	
			The guiding coalition recognizes staff for the right work in learning, collaboration, and results.	
1	2	3	**FL1. Implementation and Monitoring of the Teaching-Assessing Cycle**	
			All collaborative teams use the teaching-assessing cycle as the unit plan for all essential standards. Collaborative teams: + Screen for prior skills + Use common formative assessments + Utilize response days for prevention or extension + Give common summative assessment + Common summative assessment proficiency data to assign students to Tier 2 interventions	

1	2	3	**FL2. Identification of Essential Standards**	
			Collaborative teams have identified all essential standards for the subject or course using the REAL method (readiness, endurance, assessment, leverage). The identified essential standards do not exceed one third of the state standards.	
1	2	3	**FL3. Identification of Essential Standards**	
			Collaborative teams have identified all learning targets through deconstruction of the essential standards. All learning targets have been identified as knowledge, reasoning, skills, or products.	
1	2	3	**FL4. Instructional Rigor Aligns With State Proficiency Levels**	
			There is evidence students are exposed to quality rigorous tasks that allow them to: + Problem solve and communicate effectively both orally and through writing + Analyze and evaluate information + Show understanding	
1	2	3	**FL5. Evidence of Extended Learning for Proficient Students**	
			Students who show proficiency on the common formative or common summative assessments have identified learning targets that allow them to extend their learning in the essential standard.	
1	2	3	**C1. High-Functioning Collaborative Teams**	
			Our teacher collaborative teams are high-functioning because of the following: + Have a facilitator + Establish team roles + Establish norms + Create SMART goals based on student needs + Have agendas for the next meeting + Work interdependently while committing to teaching every student through the collaborative process + Use student data to adjust student instruction and improve teaching practices	
1	2	3	**C2. Guaranteed and Viable Curriculum**	
			All collaborative team members believe all students can learn the essential standards and commit to a guaranteed and viable curriculum for all students.	
1	2	3	**C3. Identification and Monitoring of SMART Goals**	
			All collaborative teams use SMART goals to focus on student results. The goals are monitored and used to set the direction for teachers to improve student achievement in a targeted area.	
1	2	3	**C4. Understanding 1, 5, and 10 Team Characteristics**	
			All collaborative teams understand the characteristics of a 1 team, a 5 team, and a 10 team (Mattos, 2015). All collaborative teams are monitored to ensure progress is made toward becoming a 10 team.	

Figure 3.5: Guiding coalition leadership efficacy analysis tool.

continued →

1	2	3	**C5. Identification of Future 10 Teams**	
			The guiding coalition actively seeks to identify collaborative teams that meet the A-Team characteristics and deserve A-Team system consideration.	
1	2	3	**C6. Support of Future 10 Teams**	
			The guiding coalition provides support and professional development for all collaborative teams to continue progressing to meet the standards of a 10 team.	
1	2	3	**R01. Use Data to Define the Greatest Area of Need and Give Immediate Feedback for Real-Time Instruction**	
			Collaborative teams use multiple common formative assessments to identify prevention or extension by learning targets for individual students.	
1	2	3	**R02. Create and Implement Common Summative Assessments Using Backward Design**	
			Once learning targets are established, collaborative teams create a common summative assessment before determining instructional practices and pacing. Collaborative teams use the *Design in Five* complexity ladder (Dimich, 2014) or a similar model to ensure rigor and relevance for each learning target.	
1	2	3	**R03. Common Formative Assessment Rigor and Relevance**	
			Collaborative teams create and implement common formative assessments that are in line with common summative assessments to ensure rigor and relevance.	
1	2	3	**R04: Response to Intervention Identification for Tier 2 and Tier 3**	
			Collaborative teams use a common summative assessment to identify Tier 2 students who did not meet proficiency. Guiding coalition uses a universal screener and diagnostic assessments to identify students for Tier 3 reteaching.	
1	2	3	**R05. Address Will Issues Within Tier 2**	
			The guiding coalition has established a schoolwide team of experts to work with Tier 2 students who are not proficient on the common summative assessment due to a will (not skill) issue.	
1	2	3	**R06. Address Tier 3**	
			The guiding coalition has established a schoolwide team of experts to work with Tier 3 students.	
1	2	3	**R07. Response to intervention success**	
			The guiding coalition and school intervention team regularly monitor RTI data to measure the success of Tier 2 and Tier 3 RTI programs. Data include the percentage of students entering Tiers 2 and 3 and the percent of students exiting both tiers.	

*Visit **go.SolutionTree.com/PLCbooks** for a free reproducible version of this figure.*

GUIDING COALITION ANALYSIS FOR INDIVIDUALS	
Individual Step 1: Take ten minutes to read your school's guiding coalition leadership efficacy results. Take notes on your guiding coalition analysis document.	
Team Graphic Organizer	
Team Step 1: Take twenty minutes to discuss the results of the analysis with your team.	
What results surprised you? Why?	What results affirmed your expected areas of strength and need for improvement? Why?
Team Step 2: As a team, take thirty minutes to discuss and rank the following domains by priorities of improvement. Also list your team's top five priorities of improvement from the key indicators that you can address in the 20___ to 20___ school year.		
Domain	Team Ranking 1–4 *(Top Priority of Improvement)*	Why did your team choose this ranking?
Leadership		
Focus on Learning		
Collaboration		
Results Orientation		
Top Five Key Indicators		Why did your team choose this key indicator?

Figure 3.6: Guiding coalition analysis tool for individual analysis.

*Visit **go.SolutionTree.com/PLCbooks** for a free reproducible version of this figure.*

Celebrating Guiding Coalition Leadership and Monitoring the Plan Forward

Use figure 3.7 (page 74), a tool for celebrating your leadership in the guiding coalition, to reflect on the questions effective district and school leaders ask in a PLC.

1. Are we building collective leader and teacher efficacy in our decision-making process?

2. Is there clarity in why a culture shift is needed?

3. Is there clarity in how we are going to move forward to get better results for all students?

4. Do I have a high-functioning team to provide honest feedback, address barriers to learning, and come to consensus on decisions pertaining to issues within the PLC process?

CELEBRATING YOUR LEADERSHIP Q&A	
Question	Response
If yes, how will you celebrate this important step in the PLC leadership process? If no, what steps will you take to begin the leadership transformation?	
Are we building collective leader and teacher efficacy in our decision-making process?	Yes:
	No:
Is there clarity in why a culture shift is needed?	Yes:
	No:
Is there clarity in how we are going to move forward to get better results for all students?	Yes:
	No:
Do we have a high-functioning team to provide honest feedback, address barriers to learning, and come to consensus on decisions pertaining to issues within the PLC process?	Yes:
	No:

Figure 3.7: Celebrating your leadership in the guiding coalition.

Visit *go.SolutionTree.com/PLCbooks* for a free reproducible version of this figure.

Conclusion

PLC transformation moves leadership from isolation to collaboration with the guiding coalition. The guiding coalition answers the critical PLC questions as they relate to leadership and help the team create a common language, build shared knowledge, identify and provide solutions to barriers, and, most of all, come to consensus on the why and how of the PLC journey. With their collective efficacy in the PLC process, you have an insurance policy for your leadership that will be very useful when challenges arise in the PLC culture shift. Celebrate the power in collaboration with collective responsibility for success. Use the questions (page 75) and journal prompts (page 76) to reflect on the ideas in this chapter from an organizational and then a personal viewpoint.

Chapter 3 Reflection Questions

Reflect on these questions from an organizational viewpoint.

1. Who needs to be included in helping to determine who should be a member of your guiding coalition?

2. Who needs to provide feedback and suggestions on how to celebrate staff moving into the willing and able category?

3. How have you celebrated past effective teacher leaders? Have the celebrations been focused on individual teachers or collaborative teams?

4. How can you create meaningful celebrations to acknowledge the success of a new policy, procedure, or protocol initiated by the guiding coalition?

Celebrating in a PLC at Work® © 2025 Solution Tree Press • SolutionTree.com
Visit **go.SolutionTree.com/PLCbooks** to download this free reproducible.

Chapter 3 Journal Prompts

Reflect on these questions from a personal viewpoint.

1. What is your transformational experience or experiences that have given you the wisdom, clarity, purpose, and direction to be successful?

2. How did it feel asking someone to give you honest feedback on the effectiveness of your leadership? How can you celebrate the person willing to give you honest feedback to improve your PLC leadership?

3. What characteristics do you have of a hero leader? What characteristics do you have of a host leader?

4. What areas in your PLC leadership provide you with the most satisfaction? As you become more of a host in your leadership style, how can you celebrate with other staff members to recognize the transition?

PART II

CELEBRATION OF THE BIG IDEAS

> Once a PLC has built its fundamental elements, it can focus on the first kind of 'right work' to improve student learning: the creation of a prioritized, guaranteed, and viable curriculum. A prioritized curriculum is one in which the most important standards have been identified.
>
> —Richard DuFour

CHAPTER 4

Celebrating a Focus on Learning

Extraordinary results are signified by *all* students showing proficiency or higher within a guaranteed and viable curriculum. To ensure collaborative teams are developing in a positive way, there must be a method to progress monitor the PLC maturity of each collaborative team. In the introduction (page 1), we introduced the high-functioning collaborative team core commitments that outline what is expected of high-functioning collaborative teams. This chapter focuses on the first core commitment (focus on learning) and showcases strategies of celebrating the guaranteed and viable curriculum and how highlighting the right work provides a progress-monitoring tool for collaborative teams, guiding coalitions, and system leadership in identifying essential standards, and, ultimately, a guaranteed and viable curriculum.

Ensuring a Guaranteed and Viable Curriculum

A guaranteed and viable curriculum (Marzano, 2019) is the assurance that collaboratively identified essential standards are taught to all students and that there is enough instructional time available to teach the content identified as essential. In *Leaders of Learning: How District, School, and Classroom Leaders Improve Student Achievement*, Richard DuFour and Robert J. Marzano (2011) outline the importance of a guaranteed and viable curriculum with the following statement:

> In a professional learning community, educators are committed to helping students acquire the same essential knowledge and skills regardless of the teacher to who they are assigned. Once again, the first of the big idea of a PLC is that the staff is committed to helping all students learn, and the first critical question educators in a PLC must consider in addressing that big idea is, "Learn what?" (pp. 90–91)

The first critical question of a PLC, What do we want students to know and be able to do? (DuFour et al., 2024), is an important step in establishing a guaranteed and viable curriculum. The academic standards are often numerous in number. Teachers typically are more concerned about covering each standard within the semester or school year than if their students understand the content they are teaching. This becomes a real issue for teachers who attempt to teach everything a state or provincial assessment might assess, which can affect the teacher's job security as many school districts incorporate student achievement on state assessments within teacher evaluations.

Prioritizing standards critical to student learning and success in future coursework within a guaranteed and viable curriculum ensures all students are learning at high levels. Although teachers provide instruction for each standard, it is the guarantee of proficiency on the essential standards for future success that create the winning moments for students in classroom achievement and state and national assessments. DuFour and Marzano (2011) state:

> The only way the curriculum in a school can truly be guaranteed is if the teachers themselves, those who are called upon to deliver the curriculum, have worked collaboratively to do the following:
>
> 1. Study the intended curriculum
> 2. Agree on priorities within the curriculum
> 3. Clarify how the curriculum translates into student knowledge and skills
> 4. Establish general pacing guidelines for delivering the curriculum
> 5. Commit to one another that they will, in fact, teach the agreed upon curriculum (p. 91)

This quote from DuFour and Marzano (2011) touches on several key steps in establishing a guaranteed and viable curriculum. Although in Hattie's (2009) research, teacher knowledge of subject matter effect size is low (.11 standard deviations), collaboratively studying the intended curriculum is the foundation needed before a team can prioritize standards and ultimately narrow down what is essential. This sharpens the team's ability to identify learning targets, knowledge, and skills and the pathway to pacing the instructional timeline that allows for the delivery of the essential standards. The commitment by the team to teach the collaboratively identified curriculum becomes the guaranteed and viable curriculum teams approach within a cycle of collective inquiry by asking the four critical questions (DuFour et al., 2024).

1. What knowledge, skills, and dispositions should every student acquire as a result of this unit, this course, or this grade level?
2. How will we know when each student has acquired the essential knowledge and skills?
3. How will we respond when some students do not learn?
4. How will we extend the learning for students who are already proficient? (p. 44)

The four critical questions ensure each student, regardless of teacher assigned, will have the same high levels of learning.

The expectation that students acquire the same knowledge and skills regardless of the teacher is the mindset of every high-functioning collaborative team in a PLC. In our work with collaborative teams across the United States, we consistently see the benefits of a guaranteed and viable curriculum producing extraordinary teacher performance and student achievement. The collaborative teams committed to the PLC process with a focus on learning show a tenacity for student learning of essential standards because of their efficacy in determining what students must learn and be able to do.

For example, one four-person seventh-grade mathematics team we worked with (which included a special education co-teacher) collaboratively identified their essential standards. Their team effectively provided preventions and interventions to each student as one team. Regardless of the teacher of record, a student could work with the most effective team member depending on the learning target being addressed. Their systematic instructional focus resulted in over 95 percent of their students meeting proficiency or above on each of the essential standards. Furthermore, each student had the benefit of a combined effort of four teachers to assist and extend their learning.

Mike Schmoker (2004) reminds us that "clarity proceeds competence" (p. 85). This clarity is critical during PLC transformation. A guaranteed and viable curriculum provides each team the clarity on what must be taught and allows them to focus on standards that will bring students success in future learning. Once a team identifies the essential standards, they can strategically align the support standards within the appropriate essential standard unit plan. Deciding which standards are essential or supportive is a continual process the team monitors each year. Team members adjust the essential standards as they analyze student performance data on common summative assessments, local assessments, and state and provincial assessments. This analysis provides an opportunity for celebration.

Celebrating a Focus on Learning and the Guaranteed and Viable Curriculum

Using figure I.1 (page 4) as the framework, we will now outline examples of how to celebrate high-functioning collaborative teams demonstrating a focus on learning. Following are the indicators on the rubric for focus on learning.

Core Commitment 1: Focus on Learning Strand

1. We have worked through the REAL process for determining readiness, endurance, assessment, and leverage to properly identify the essential standards for our subject area.

2. We have identified appropriate learning targets with learning progressions as key components of the essential standard, and our instructional planning is geared to ensure students meet proficiency, including prevention, intervention, and reteaching.

3. We have outlined the sequencing and pacing for each essential standard and illustrated our prevention, intervention, and reteaching strategies.

4. We have developed our common summative assessments and corresponding common formative assessments establishing appropriate proficiency and DOK levels through data-driven analysis.

5. Our instructional techniques are rigorous research-based strategies fostering high student performance on common summative assessments, MAP, Milestones, and other assessment platforms.

The following sections expand on these indicators.

REAL Process

The REAL process (Ainsworth, 2015) helps teams determine essential standards. It measures a standard's readiness, endurance, assessment, and leverage.

- **Readiness:** Does the standard prepare students for success at the next level (grade, course, or unit)?

- **Endurance:** Does the standard endure beyond this one skill or unit?

- **Assessment (in external exams):** Will this standard prepare students for success on a high-stakes external exam?

- **Leverage:** Will the skills and concepts learned with this standard extend beyond this course and unit? Will they cross into other courses or disciplines?

It is recommended that collaborative teams follow these or similar questions when determining essential standards in the guaranteed and viable curriculum, which builds collective teacher efficacy. Bypassing this step and assigning the content standards to teachers erodes teacher efficacy in determining what is essential for students to learn.

To properly identify the essential standards, the team must first deconstruct each standard to ensure they have clarity on what standards require students to know and be able to do. With clarity on each standard, the team works through the REAL process to establish their essential standards. Once this is done, the team monitors the level of priority of the essential standards through student performance data on the formative and summative assessments, as well as state assessments. Based on vertical collaboration and state assessment results, the team adjusts essential standards each year to ensure students are prepared for success at the next grade or course level, are learning information required for more than one skill, have the knowledge to demonstrate proficiency on high-stakes assessments, and have the required skills to be successful in other disciplines.

A frequent response of teachers and leaders beginning the PLC process is "Wouldn't it be more efficient to give collaborative teams a list of the essential standards?" Our research and practice indicate the process of collaboratively identifying essential standards with a systematic process by the team provides the teacher investment required to passionately pursue each student showing proficiency or above on every essential standard and provides a great opportunity for celebration. Debating and critically analyzing standards and content to accurately determine what is essential provides depth of understanding. This clarity about the standards leads to competency in teaching the learning targets. Once the teachers complete the process of identifying their essential standards and learning targets, they are better prepared to make more effective instructional adjustments to meet student needs.

Identifying Essential Standards

Identifying the collaborative teams that have early success in identifying essential standards allows the superintendent and principal to showcase the teams' work. At the district level, board meetings provide a great opportunity for high-functioning teams to present their essential standards process. This recognition keeps the board members and community stakeholders aware of the school's academic framework and reinforces the right work to collaborative teams across the school district. The attention to teams who have identified the essential standards allows leadership to monitor those teams who have not met this key action step and provide the support needed for the team to establish their guaranteed curriculum.

Opportunities at district-level leadership meetings and school staff meetings are valuable times to celebrate and showcase the essential standards process. It is powerful to have a high-functioning collaborative team describe in detail how they established their essential standards using the REAL process in front of leaders from across the school district. These presentations motivate school leaders to inspire their staff to skillfully identify their essential standards.

This district approach can be modeled at the local school as well. Any time a staff is together is an opportunity to have local teachers showcase the right work. Allowing time for collaborative teams to walk through the REAL process with their peers is effective in inspiring staff to get on board. This message can be further communicated through posting essential standards by team in strategic areas of the school or within the professional development room or data room.

To celebrate selection and implementation of the guaranteed and viable curriculum, collaborative teams can share their development processes. Pictures that share the story of the selection process are great motivators to other teams that may be struggling. It is strategically smart to allow successful teams time to explain how they navigated the selection process and what barriers they overcame to come to consensus. Figure 4.1 (page 84) provides a template schools and districts can use to showcase collaborative teams' work in identifying their essential standards and ultimately their guaranteed and viable curriculum. The template can also serve as a progress-monitoring tool as each team must complete this key step in establishing a high-functioning PLC.

CELEBRATION: FOCUS ON LEARNING				
Our team successfully identified the following essential standards or skills for our guaranteed and viable curriculum.				
Collaborative Team:		**Subject:**		
REAL Indicator	**Readiness** *Does the standard or skill prepare students for the next level?*	**Endurance** *Does the standard have endurance?*	**Assessment** *Will the standard prepare students for success on high-stakes external exams?*	**Leverage** *Does the standard have leverage?*
Standard or Skill	For each standard or skill, mark the appropriate indicators.			

Source for REAL: Ainsworth, 2015.

Figure 4.1: Collaborative team REAL celebration tool.

*Visit **go.SolutionTree.com/PLCbooks** for a free reproducible version of this figure.*

Essential Standards Workshop

For a district with multiple schools at each level, it is important to have a guaranteed and viable curriculum not only within each school, but also across the school district. Once teams establish their essential standards and are comfortable with the process, the next step is getting a districtwide perspective. To accomplish and celebrate a systemic guaranteed and viable curriculum, we suggest an essential standards workshop.

For this example, we use a workshop that includes English language arts, mathematics, science, and social studies content that is connected to a state assessment. In preparation for the essential standards workshop, collaborative teams completed the following questions and the form in figure 4.2 for each of their identified essential standards.

1. Why did you deem your selected standards as essential?
2. When and how did you progress monitor?
3. How did your team address targets that need additional instruction?
4. What targets could stretch students' learning even further?
5. Should this remain an essential standard?
6. Do any adjustments need to be made to the learning targets?
7. If this is a yearlong standard, how are you progress monitoring?

ESSENTIAL STANDARDS WORKSHOP PREWORK	
Directions: Each collaborative team shoud complete the template for each identified essential standard.	
Essential Standard	**Grade or Subject**
Readiness	**Endurance**
Reasoning or Evidence	**Reasoning or Evidence**

Source for REAL : Ainsworth, 2015.
Figure 4.2: Essential standards workshop prework.

continued →

Assessment	Leverage
Reasoning or Evidence	Reasoning or Evidence

Learning Targets

Prerequiste Knowledge and Skills and Vocabulary

Provide a sample question that demonstrates proficiency at the appropriate DOK level.

*Visit **go.SolutionTree.com/PLCbooks** for a free reproducible version of this figure.*

The workshop occurs in two sessions. The first session involves each team sharing their local school collaborative team's list of essential standards and rationale for their decisions using figure 4.2 for each essential standard. Every essential standard identified is added to a new district list for that grade level or subject. From the newly developed district list of essential standards, the group discusses and comes to consensus on a list of the most essential standards based on district consensus. This discussion occurs during the afternoon session. To ensure collective teacher efficacy throughout the school district, the newly recommended district essential standards lists are taken back to each collaborative team in the individual school using the template in figure 4.3 for further discussion and consensus. During preplanning each school year, the collaborative team leaders reconvene to discuss and update any essential standards as deemed necessary from the review process.

CELEBRATION: SYSTEM ESSENTIAL STANDARDS				
Our system identified the following essential standards and skills for our guaranteed and viable curriculum.				
Subject or Course:				
REAL Indicator	Readiness *Does the standard or skill prepare students for the next level?*	Endurance *Does the standard have endurance?*	Assessment *Will the standard prepare students for success on high-stakes external exams?*	Leverage *Does the standard have leverage?*
Standard or Skill	For each standard or skill, mark the appropriate indicators.			

Figure 4.3: Essential standards workshop celebration tool.

*Visit **go.SolutionTree.com/PLCbooks** for a free reproducible version of this figure.*

The essential standards workshop serves as a celebration of the school district's commitment to a guaranteed and viable curriculum and an effective progress-monitoring tool. The essential standards workshop demonstrates the district's commitment to the PLC process and increases each teacher's skill in identifying essential standards. The workshop provides district leadership an opportunity to celebrate the wins in a critical area of a PLC and monitor the progress of each collaborative team in identifying their essential standards. The recognition confirms that the teachers' work is important to the future success of all students in the school district. It is a powerful moment when the superintendent praises this work at a school board meeting and can exclaim the school district has a guaranteed and viable curriculum for all students regardless of a student's neighborhood or street address.

Collaborative Team Impact Checks

For school districts or schools to monitor PLC progress and provide meaningful feedback and celebration of practices, we recommend a collaborative team impact check. These checks can be led by central office staff and local school administrators, academic staff, and teachers. Collaborative team impact checks are scheduled throughout the year and provide professional learning feedback and progress monitoring for collaborative teams, the school's guiding coalition, and the school district. The template in figure 4.4 provides examples of best practices for collaboration and key actions teams complete around the four critical questions that drive their PLC work along with multiple sections to identify actions to celebrate. The first core commitment, a focus on learning, seeks evidence of appropriate learning targets and learning progressions, pacing guides, common assessments, and rigor that are key actions in attaining a guaranteed and viable curriculum.

PLC COLLABORATION IMPACT CHECK							
School:			**Date:**		**Collaboration Time:**		
Focus:			**Team:**		**Observer:**		
Team Structures	Yes	No	N/A	Focus	Yes	No	N/A
				What do students need to know and be able to do?			
Uses agenda				Deconstructing standards			
Establishes team norms				Identifying essential standards			
Follows and enforces team norms				Writing learning targets			
Assigns team roles				Establishing pacing guides			
Maximizes use of collaborative time				Planning instructional strategies			
Expects contributions from each team member							

Areas in need of development:	Celebrations:			
	How will we know when students have learned it?			
	Aligns common summative assessments to essential standards			
	Creates common formative assessments collaboratively			
	Builds common understanding of proficiency			
	Clarifies conditions of administration			
	Compares and analyzes data			
	Celebrations:			
Overall Celebrations:				
	What will we do when students have not learned it?			
	Plan interventions			
	Plan to provide timely response to students			
	Plan to differentiate to meet students' needs			
	Celebrations:			
	What will we do when students already know it?			
	Plan to provide extension activities			
	Plan to extend instruction			
	Plan to differentiate to meet needs			
	Celebrations:			

Figure 4.4: Collaborative team impact check form.

*Visit **go.SolutionTree.com/PLCbooks** for a free reproducible version of this figure.*

In *Design in Five*, Nicole Dimich (2014) states that "learning goals (targets) tightly align to the standards, representing the learning students need to reflect the essence of the standards" (p. 27). Learning targets are often written in student-friendly language to provide clarity to the students and teachers on the desired outcomes of the lesson. There are four types of learning targets.

1. **Knowledge:** These are facts and concepts we want students to know.
2. **Reasoning:** These targets use what students know to reason and solve problems.
3. **Skills:** These targets use student knowledge and reasoning to act skillfully.
4. **Products:** With these targets, students use knowledge, reasoning, and skills to create a concrete product.

High-functioning collaborative teams embrace this step by further organizing their learning targets in order of complexity. As outlined in *Design in Five* (Dimich, 2014), the learning targets are placed in order of complexity up the progression ladder. The bottom rungs of the ladder are less complex learning targets. The middle of the ladder lists learning targets students must understand to show proficiency of the standard. The top of the ladder are targets that equate to exceeding the standard. The learning targets from the essential standard are separated into three levels by complexity: (1) prerequisite learning targets, (2) required by the standard learning targets, and (3) extension learning targets.

Pacing guides set the pathway for collaborative teams to meet the instructional demands of teaching each essential standard and supporting standards. Once the team has established their essential standards, they can better organize their instructional timeline to ensure all students meet proficiency or higher on the guaranteed and viable curriculum. Jane L. David (2008) writes that "the best pacing guides emphasize curricular guidance instead of prescriptive pacing. . . . Constructive pacing guides assume differences in teachers, students, and school contexts. They adjust expectations through frequent revisions based on input from teachers." The collaborative team must have autonomy in determining their pacing guides and use results on common formative assessments to measure their pacing. For example, if less than 75 percent of students are not meeting proficiency on the common formative assessments, then the pacing may have to slow down, and new instructional strategies need to be considered.

High-functioning collaborative teams develop common summative assessments and corresponding common formative assessments. Cassandra Erkens (2014a) outlines three reasons why teams need common summative assessments. The first reason is common summative assessments center teams on what needs to be accomplished with their instruction, curriculum, and assessments. Second, summative assessments answer the question, What do you know at this moment in time? Its purpose is to certify learning, and it is comprehensive, putting all the little steps together in meaningful ways. Third, success breeds success and an increased sense of hope and efficacy. Common formative assessments are the building blocks toward the common summative assessment. High-functioning teams use formative assessments as stepping stones for students who must meet proficiency or above before attempting the common summative assessment.

At the completion of identifying the essential standards, the team creates an assessment plan for each unit starting with the common summative assessment. Utilizing a backward design, the team starts with the summative assessment, ensuring each learning target is appropriately addressed in the assessment. Using the learning target sequence of the unit, the collaborative team creates a common formative assessment for each learning target. Teams determine and justify the level of proficiency for each common assessment and articulate how the assessment measures the student's understanding of the knowledge and skills of the learning target.

In *Unstoppable Learning*, Douglas Fisher and Nancy Frey (2015) characterize rigor as the balance between complexity and difficulty. In *Design in Five*, Nicole Dimich (2014) writes, "Quality rigorous tasks involve our students in taking concepts we want them to learn and asking them to—individually and in collaboration with peers—evaluate, analyze, and problem solve" (pp. 44–45).

High-functioning collaborative teams show how their instructional techniques are rigorous research-based strategies fostering high student performance on common summative assessments, MAP, Milestones, and other assessment platforms. They are asked to provide relevant student achievement data demonstrating high levels of learning for all students.

When using figure 4.4 (page 88), each collaborative team is observed by a team, with evidence documented on the rubric. The observation team can be made up of teachers, academic support staff, and administrators from within the school system as well as district leadership. A check is marked in the boxes if the criteria was seen by the observation team. Upon conclusion of the observations, the leader calculates the observed percentage of the collected information. For example, using figure 4.4 (page 88), if the observed collaborative team showed evidence of their list of identified essential standards, the observer would put a check in the box on the form.

At the completion of the observations, the team calculates all the data collected from each category. Each member of the team compiles their data and adds the amount to the overall group. Once all the data are compiled, the group shares suggested areas of growth and outlines areas of celebration for each category. By design, the collaborative team impact check celebrates positive behaviors from the form as well as areas of growth. This process reinforces the right work of collaborative teams while providing valuable feedback on how the district or school's PLC implementation plan is evolving.

Conclusion

Celebrating the small wins and breakthroughs of collaborative teacher teams allows the district or school to reinforce the PLC expectations, monitor how well collaborative teams are functioning, and provide future professional learning opportunities. Successful celebrations signify small wins that all staff members can achieve to serve as a continuation of successfully accomplishing the work deemed most important for the school culture. Ensure your celebrations support what you value most from the building blocks of your success to the highest-functioning teams serving as evidence of what the right work looks like. As leaders, we need to have celebrations of success; however, we need to prioritize celebrations for success. Use the questions (page 92) and journal prompts (page 93) to reflect on the ideas in this chapter from an organizational and then a personal viewpoint.

Chapter 4 Reflection Questions

Reflect on the following questions from an organizational viewpoint.

1. What is our current reality in establishing and implementing a guaranteed and viable curriculum?

___

2. What processes of the guaranteed and viable curriculum can we currently celebrate?

___

3. What processes of the guaranteed and viable curriculum do we need to strengthen through celebration?

___

4. Who needs to provide feedback and suggestions on how to celebrate our guaranteed and viable curriculum?

___

5. Identify the most appropriate time and place to celebrate the staff's work supporting a guaranteed and viable curriculum.

___

Chapter 4 Journal Prompts

Reflect on these questions from a personal viewpoint.

1. How can you increase your understanding and implementation of a guaranteed and viable curriculum?

2. How can you become more actively engaged in your team or school in guaranteeing that all students learn at high levels the essential standards?

3. In your role, how have you celebrated your team's success around a focus on learning?

The powerful paradigm that we are much more effective together than we are separately drives the entire PLC process.

—**Anthony Muhammad**

CHAPTER 5

Celebrating Collaboration and Collective Responsibility

In chapter 4 (page 79), we examined how a team's focus on learning is built on ensuring a guaranteed and viable curriculum. The establishment of a guaranteed and viable curriculum is critical in providing collaborative teams with a clear purpose for their work. In this chapter, we illustrate how local schools and school systems can celebrate the right work (the collaborative work and collective responsibility) of high-functioning teacher teams, which is the engine that will push schools toward all students being proficient or higher on the essential standards. We will also connect how recognition is a tool for leaders and teachers to progress monitor the culture shift from isolation to collaboration.

In our experience, success is typically not tied only to the actions of one person. Deeper accomplishment is due to the collaborative effort of a team. As Jenni Donohoo, John Hattie, and Rachel Eells (2018) share, efficacy is one of the most impactful strategies on student learning; *collective teacher efficacy*, they state, is the belief that "when a team of individuals share the belief that through their unified efforts they can overcome challenges and produce intended results, groups *are* more effective." Teacher collective efficacy is the energy that gives teams the ability to break through their students' learning barriers.

The second big idea of a PLC is working collaboratively with colleagues. DuFour (2004) considers collaboration powerful once it becomes systematic and focuses on the analysis of data to improve classroom practice.

> The powerful collaboration that characterizes professional learning communities is a systematic process in which teachers work together to analyze and improve their classroom practice. Teachers work in teams, engaging in an ongoing cycle of questions that promote deep team learning. This process, in turn, leads to higher levels of student achievement. (p. 8)

Evidence has shown that working collaboratively is best practice. Collaboration in its truest sense promotes authentic team learning, which leads to improved student achievement. Through collaboration, teachers can lead sustainable change and impact student learning far beyond their own classrooms.

In our experience leading a Model PLC school system and from our work with schools across the United States, we know that ensuring the collaborative teams are focused on the right work is critical in creating a strong PLC culture where students achieve at higher levels. DuFour and colleagues (2024) aptly note the fact that simple teacher collaboration will do nothing to improve a school. They point out that "the pertinent question is not, 'Are they collaborating?' but rather, what are they collaborating about?'" (DuFour et al., 2024, p. 59). In this chapter, we will outline important actions of high-functioning collaborative teams and present tools to use to celebrate the right work of teams while providing a window into how teams are progressing in their collaboration effectiveness.

Celebrating a Collaborative Culture and Collective Responsibility

As a point of reference for this chapter, we will look to the characteristics from figure I.1 (page 4), which lists actions of high-functioning collaborative teams. Core commitment two: collaborative culture and collective responsibility focuses on the effective behaviors and procedures around the second big idea of a PLC. In this chapter, we will illustrate how a school or system can celebrate these qualities, and we will present tools to use in identifying collaborative teams meeting these expectations. The templates are also an effective progress-monitoring tool for collaboration and collective responsibility. Following are the indicators for collaborative culture and collective responsibility.

1. We have identified team norms and protocols identifying student learning as a focus to guide us in working collaboratively.

2. We have established a collegial environment where all members participate and have a connection and understanding of all our students we serve. Each member can articulate all aspects of the PLC process.

3. We have established roles and responsibilities where all members have accountability toward student learning. Responsibilities are distributed to team members to address intervention and extension activities, and evidence of those implemented instructional strategies are observable.

4. We have a pervasive culture of collaboratively evaluating student work, sharing effective instructional strategies, sharing what strategies did not work, and assessing prerequisite skills.

5. When facing an obstacle of learning, collaboration, and results unique to our team, we develop strategies and processes to overcome the barriers.

Collaboration: What Does It Look, Sound, and Feel Like?

We have found through our professional development experiences that educators need a visual point of reference to further their understanding of what a collaborative meeting should look like. In one circumstance, we were asked by a principal to illustrate what a collaborative team meeting looks, sounds, and feels like with the purpose of providing his staff an exemplar to work from to improve collaboration. In response to that request, we looked toward our high-functioning collaborative teams within our school system to provide a description.

As noted in the introduction to this book (page 1), the Bartow County School System developed an award that collaborative teams could receive who meet certain PLC criteria (see figure I.1 [page 4] for the application criteria). The high-functioning teams also must show evidence of student learning. To show what a collaborative meeting should look, feel, and sound like, we combined our knowledge of these award-winning high-functioning collaborative teams from each level—elementary, middle, and high school—and asked them to provide their expertise in responding to these questions. Each of the high-functioning collaborative teams also worked at a Model PLC school.

Figure 5.1 outlines the responses from the high-functioning collaborative teams to the question, What does it look like? Figure 5.2 (page 98) outlines the responses from the high-functioning collaborative teams to the question, What does it sound like? Figure 5.3 (page 98) outlines responses from the high-functioning collaborative teams to the question, What does it feel like?

WHAT COLLABORATION LOOKS LIKE	
Engaged Setting	Team members are seated strategically in preparation to actively participate.
Organized	All members of the team know their role and steps in the process. Protocols, agendas, and procedures are present and observed.
Prepared	All members have their evidence of student learning from the common formative assessment and are ready to share their results.
Data, Charts, and Numbers	The team creates unifying data sources to easily cite information for SMART goals, instructional adjustments, strengths, areas of growth, and so on.
Specific	Data are student by student and skill by skill. Subgroups are discussed and identified.
Consistent	The assessment or task being analyzed is the same across the team.

Figure 5.1: What does collaboration look like?

*Visit **go.SolutionTree.com/PLCbooks** for a free reproducible version of this figure.*

WHAT COLLABORATION SOUNDS LIKE	
Intentional	Time is not wasted on outside noise or sidebar conversations. Conversations focus on the agenda at hand with one voice.
Common Language	You hear a common use of key terms of the PLC process such as *prevention*, *intervention*, and *reteaching* within the RTI process. Teams use *our* versus *my*.
Productive Tone	Voice inflection is clear, professional, and responsive to the task at hand.
Thought-Provoking Discussion	Discussions are welcomed and encouraged in seeking solutions to learning barriers without assigning blame.
Consensus on Proficiency	There is collegial debate and discussion on what proficiency is.

Figure 5.2: What does collaboration sound like?

*Visit **go.SolutionTree.com/PLCbooks** for a free reproducible version of this figure.*

WHAT COLLABORATION FEELS LIKE	
Collaborative	There is a feeling of flexibility toward doing the right work to impact student learning.
Confident	Team members are confident in one another because of their intentional focus on learning.
Optimistic	The process is encouraging to team members due to systematic interventions.
Calm	There isn't any panic as members are confident in the process and have experienced positive results.
Trust	There is an atmosphere of support for each member to be successful.
Collegial Spirit	You can sense the drive for all students learning at high levels.
Openness	There is a spirit of transparency within the team and for outside support.

Figure 5.3: What does collaboration feel like?

*Visit **go.SolutionTree.com/PLCbooks** for a free reproducible version of this figure.*

Learning from practitioners within an established effective PLC culture is a good strategy we recommend for educators who are just starting the PLC journey or trying to perfect their own PLC practices. In this spirit, we utilized the specific responses from the high-functioning team members and organized them into a rubric. Figure 5.4 provides specific descriptions that help paint a picture of strong collaboration practices.

WHAT HIGH-FUNCTIONING COLLABORATIVE TEAMS LOOK, SOUND, AND FEEL LIKE					
1 = Not Evident; 2 = In Progress; 3 = Embedded in Our Culture					
Indicator	Description	Rating		
What High-Functioning Collaborative Teams Look Like					
Engaged Setting	Team members are seated strategically in preparation to actively participate.	1	2	3
Organized	All members of the team know their role and steps in the process. Protocols, agendas, and procedures are present and observed.	1	2	3
Prepared	All members have their evidence of student learning from the common formative assessment and are ready to share their results.	1	2	3
Data, Charts, and Numbers	The team creates unifying data sources to easily cite information for SMART goals, instructional adjustments, strengths, areas of growth, and so on.	1	2	3
Specific	Data are student by student and skill by skill. Subgroups are discussed and identified.	1	2	3
Consistent	The assessment or task being analyzed is the same across the team.	1	2	3
What High-Functioning Collaborative Teams Sound Like					
Intentional	Time is not wasted on outside noise or sidebar conversations. Conversations focus on the agenda at hand with one voice.	1	2	3
Common Language	You hear a common use of key terms of the PLC process such as *prevention*, *intervention*, and *reteaching* within the RTI process.	1	2	3
Productive Tone	Voice inflection is clear, professional, and responsive to the task at hand.	1	2	3
Thought-Provoking Discussion	Discussions are welcomed and encouraged in seeking solutions to learning barriers without assigning blame.	1	2	3
Consensus on Proficiency	There is collegial debate and discussion on what proficiency is.	1	2	3
What High-Functioning Collaborative Teams Feel Like					
Collaborative	There is a feeling of flexibility toward doing the right work to impact learning.	1	2	3
Confident	Team members are confident in one another because of their intentional focus.	1	2	3
Optimistic	The process is encouraging to team members due to systematic interventions.	1	2	3
Calm	There isn't any panic as members are confident in the process and have experienced positive results.	1	2	3
Trust	There is an atmosphere of support for each member to be successful.	1	2	3
Collegial Spirit	You can sense the drive for all students learning at high levels.	1	2	3
Openness	There is a spirit of transparency within the team and for outside support.	1	2	3

Figure 5.4: What high-functioning collaborative teams look, sound, and feel like.

*Visit **go.SolutionTree.com/PLCbooks** for a free reproducible version of this figure.*

The rubric provides a reference point of best practices for novice teams as they begin to develop their collaborative team habits and for more experienced teams who want to sharpen their practices. More specifically, in the "What High-Functioning Collaborative Teams Look Like" section, the message is around preparation, organization, and consistency. Strong teams are intentional in the way they are seated during the meeting, how their data are presented, and the roles that each member leads during the meeting. The message from the "What High-Functioning Collaborative Teams Sound Like" section is the consistency of the language used during the meeting and the tone of the discussion. High-functioning teams have productive discussion with the goal of seeking solutions, not blame. In the last section, "What High-Functioning Collaborative Teams Feel Like," there is a feeling of confidence in the process that is fostered by trust and openness between the team members.

The tool can be used for self-reflection for a collaborative team or as a feedback instrument by a school leader or outside representative, such as a local or central office academic staff member. Each specific indicator can be rated at three different levels: (1) not evident, (2) in progress, and (3) embedded in our culture. If a team has an overall score averaging between 1.5 and 2.5, the team is considered in progress toward becoming a high-functioning collaborative team. A team that scores above 2.5 would be considered at a level where high-functioning collaboration practices are embedded in their culture. A team who scores below a 1.5 has a high number of key indicators that are not evident or in progress within their collaborative team culture.

As a school or district develops their PLC culture, figure 5.4 (page 99) can be an effective tool in celebrating the right work of collaborative teams. It is our suggestion that the tool be used first as a reflective tool for the team. As they develop their collaborative team practices, they can monitor their growth through self-rating in each area as they work toward embedding the specifics of each indicator into their culture. Once the team meets the 2.5 or above standard based on their self-reflection, we recommend an outside team of observers from the local school staff, members of the school's guiding coalition, or central office academic leaders conduct one or more observations of the team and provide feedback on the template. This validates their work and provides valuable feedback for improvement from an outside independent perspective.

What is critical and the central theme of this book is the next step that we often neglect in our implementation process. As teams reach a level of collaboration where effective practices are embedded in their collaborative team culture, take time to celebrate their accomplishments in a meaningful and public way with the staff, community, and central office leadership. Capture the team's rubric rating on a well-placed bulletin board or high-traffic space for all to see. Celebrate the team at the next staff meeting by specifically announcing their accomplishment in meeting the characteristics of what high-performing teams look, sound, and feel like.

Another form of celebration is to ask the team to present their successes to their peers. Teachers learn well from other teachers. Providing opportunities for teachers to showcase their strategies of sound collaborative team practices is an effective professional development strategy. Keeping good practices in isolation is counter to the big ideas of a PLC.

Collaborative Culture and Collective Responsibility Success Criteria

In *Visible Learning for Teachers*, John Hattie (2012) examines how success criteria are a powerful way to impact student learning. When students have clarity in the expectations for the task at hand, they are "more likely to work toward mastering the criteria of success, more likely to know where they are on the trajectory towards this success and have a good chance of learning how to monitor and self-regulate their progress" (Hattie, 2012, p. 67). With this in mind, we set out to create success criteria for our teachers in implementing the PLC process. We developed our high-functioning collaborative team rubric for each of the three big ideas as presented in the introduction of the book in figure I.1 (page 1).

Using *Learning by Doing* (DuFour et al., 2024) as our guide and Mike Mattos's (2015) 1-5-10 team strategy as our inspiration, we created a high-functioning team rubric. In its original version, the rubric specifically outlined five strands for each of the big ideas of the PLC process. Each strand represents key actions of high-functioning PLCs.

As we implemented our high-functioning team rubric throughout our school system, we noted some inconsistencies in how collaborative teams were interpreting and conducting each strand of the rubric. These inconsistencies gave us two vital pieces of information. One, we needed to strengthen our common language and clarify our expectations to ensure consistency in practice. Two, the rubric shed light on our progress in our PLC culture shift.

To strengthen our common language and clarify our expectations, we leaned on practitioners of the PLC process. Our system guiding coalition and local school academic leaders were asked to complete this task of creating success criteria for our high-functioning teams rubric. The team consisted of principals for each school, instructional lead teachers and learning support strategists from each school, and central office executive cabinet members and academic leaders.

Inspired from this collaborative effort, figure 5.5 (page 102) is a rubric specifically targeted toward establishing highly effective collaborative teams. Along with the strands, success criteria for each area provide specific information and steps that are needed for teams to become high functioning.

COLLABORATIVE CULTURE AND COLLECTIVE RESPONSIBILITY SUCCESS CRITERIA PROGRESS-MONITORING AND CELEBRATION TOOL		
1 = Not evident; 3 = In progress; 5 = Embedded in our culture		
Indicator	**Success Criteria**	**Rating**
We have identified team norms and protocols identifying student learning as a focus to guide us in working collaboratively.	We identified team norms focused on student learning.	1
	Our norms address the four critical questions.	
	We identified protocols for norm violations.	3
	We review norms at the beginning of each meeting.	
	We review norms and violations periodically and update as needed.	5
We have established a collegial environment where all members participate and have a connection and understanding of all the students we serve. Each member can articulate all aspects of the PLC process.	We trust each other as professionals.	1
	We established clear roles.	
	We follow norms and accountability steps.	
	We take responsibility for all students.	3
	We plan Tier 1 prevention and Tier 2 interventions.	
	We include support staff in collaboration as appropriate.	
	We are engaged during collaboration.	5
	We use correct PLC vocabulary.	
We have established roles and responsibilities where all members have an accountability toward student learning and team members address intervention and extension activities, and evidence of those implemented instructional strategies are observable.	We analyze common summative assessment data by learning target to determine: + Which students need intervention or extension + Which instructional strategies were most successful	1
		3
	We designate team members responsible for intervention or extension based on data.	5
We have a pervasive culture of collaboratively evaluating student work, sharing effective instructional strategies, sharing what strategies did not work, and assessing prerequisite skills.	We use the idea of *our* students, not *my* students.	1
	We score common formative and common summative assessments collaboratively.	
	We are transparent about results.	
	We are open to changing strategies based on data.	3
	We trust each other throughout the collaboration process.	
	We share students during Tier 2 intervention.	5
	We document strategies being used to drive reflection.	
When facing an obstacle of learning, collaboration, and results unique to our team, we develop strategies and processes to overcome the barriers.	We can discuss and provide written commentary displaying our instructional agility.	1
	We have a norm addressing barriers.	3
	We use support staff when barriers arise.	5
Celebrate teams who score a 22 or higher as an example of the right work.		Total:

Figure 5.5: Collaborative culture and collective responsibility success criteria.

*Visit **go.SolutionTree.com/PLCbooks** for a free reproducible version of this figure.*

The first strand of figure 5.5 focuses on identifying norms and protocols where student learning is the primary goal of the team. The following is the list of success criteria.

- We identified team norms focused on student learning. Norms address the four guiding questions.
- We identified protocols for norm violations.
- We review norms at the beginning of each meeting.
- We review norms and violations periodically and update as needed.

In our experience, norms are often limited to addressing adult behavior. We encourage teams to expand their thinking and incorporate key PLC concepts and actions. For example, the following norm ties in key terms within the PLC process: We will provide systems of support to ensure our students are proficient or above on the guaranteed and viable curriculum. It is also important for a team to develop protocols to address norm violations. The violation protocols can begin with a simple gesture such as a tap on the watch or a visual sign to address a violation. If the behavior continues, the violation protocol may progress toward a one-to-one conversation between the team facilitator and the violator and ultimately an administrator if behavior does not stop.

The second strand of figure 5.5 centers on the culture of the team and their familiarity with the PLC process. The following is the list of success criteria.

- We trust each other as professionals.
- We established clear roles.
- We follow norms and accountability steps.
- We take responsibility for all students.
- We plan Tier 1 prevention and Tier 2 interventions.
- We include support staff in collaboration as appropriate.
- We are engaged during collaboration.
- We use correct PLC vocabulary.

A high-functioning team should have a level of trust between its members. There should be documented roles for each member of the team that they are held accountable for fulfilling. The members should use the language of the PLC process that is consistent and established by their guiding coalition. Their preparation for Tier 1 prevention strategies and Tier 2 intervention strategies must be connected to a deep understanding of the students they serve.

The third strand of figure 5.5 focuses the team's responsibility to their students' achievement and each member utilizing the agreed-on strategies to intervene and extend the students on the essential standards and learning targets. The following is the list of success criteria.

- We analyze common summative assessment data by learning target to determine:
  - → Which students need intervention or extension
  - → Which instructional strategies were most successful
- We designate team members responsible for intervention or extension based on data.

High-functioning collaborative teams follow data protocols to identify the students who met or did not meet proficiency on their common assessments. The team then divides the responsibility of the members to provide intervention and extension activities in their effort to ensure all of their students are learning at high levels.

The fourth strand of figure 5.5 (page 102) focuses on collectively evaluating student work and sharing best practices. The following is the list of success criteria.

- We score common summative and common formative assessments collaboratively.
- We are transparent about results.
- We are open to changing strategies based on data.
- We trust each other throughout the collaboration process.
- We share students during Tier 2 intervention.
- We document strategies being used to drive reflection.

PLCs are not only about student learning, but they are also about adult learning. In *Leverage: Using PLCs to Promote Lasting Improvement in Schools*, Thomas W. Many and Susan K. Sparks-Many (2014) write:

> When teachers work together on collaborative teams, they improve their practice in two important ways. First, they sharpen their pedagogy by sharing specific instructional strategies for teaching more effectively. Second, they deepen their content knowledge by identifying the specific standards students must master. In other words, when teachers work together, they become better teachers. (p. 83)

The best professional development happens during collaborative teams' time together. Members of a high-functioning team are transparent about their student learning data and are open to changing their practices if the data suggest adjustment is needed. One particular high-functioning team that we had the honor of observing called the movement of students between teachers for intervention "shuffling." The members would shuffle their students among the team members so often that the students felt like they had a team of mathematics teachers instead of just one. The team's percentage of proficient or higher on the state milestone was the highest in the school system.

The fifth strand of figure 5.5 (page 102) is all about the team's ability to overcome their students' learning obstacles. The following is the list of success criteria.

- We can discuss and provide written commentary displaying our instructional agility.
- We have a norm addressing barriers.
- We use support staff when barriers arise.

High-performing collaborative teams overcome learning obstacles with a unified approach. Because of their commitment to a guaranteed and viable curriculum, they are open to implementing more effective learning strategies when their own strategies did not work. Their meetings are open to local support staff and system instructional support personnel. Once again, all students, not just "*my* students," attaining high levels of learning is the goal.

In *Transforming School Culture*, Anthony Muhammad (2018) writes, "How schools celebrate learning and those who help students learn says a lot about how much the school values learning" (p. 126). The collaborative culture and collective responsibility success criteria are a tool to help leaders celebrate the right work of collaborative teams where learning is the primary focus. The tool can act as a self-reflective instrument of the team's progress in collaboration, and it can be used by local leaders as a monitoring tool on the level of progress their collaborative teams are making on the implementation of key collaborative team actions. With the ultimate goal of becoming a high-functioning collaborative team, a team that accomplishes a cumulative score of 22 or above would be considered high-performing and an exemplar of the right work.

Celebrate the success of teams that score a 22 or higher for success criteria. A staff meeting is a great opportunity to publicly acknowledge a collaborative team that excels in collaboration. Social media is another effective way to celebrate a team. In our school system, local schools were very intentional in celebrating their effective collaborative teams through multiple social media platforms. Social media show pictures and narratives of collaborative teams in various stages of the collaborative team process. In one circumstance, we filmed a third-grade team showcasing their process for analyzing student data. Their collegial tone captured key actions outlined in our success criteria for collaboration. Documenting their team success and highlighting it through our school system website not only validated and celebrated their work, but it also provided an exemplar of excellence that others could see. Videos like these are also a great learning tool.

Leading professional learning is another excellent way to celebrate the good work of collaborative teams. We have accomplished this strategy in two ways. First, our high-functioning collaborative teams provide professional development for new teachers. We allow time each year for new teachers to be a part of a professional learning session on PLCs specifically in the area of collaboration led by our most successful collaborative teams. It is one of the highlights of the new teacher orientation as documented through their evaluation surveys of the orientation. Each presenting team is introduced to the incoming class of new teachers as the best of the best. The pride and excitement are on full display as the team works with the new teachers.

The second way we celebrate our teams through professional development is when outside school system representatives visit our schools to see our PLC process in action. One of the highlights of the visit for the groups is seeing high-functioning collaborative teams in action. Once again, our teachers love to be observed and answer questions about the process they are committed to every day. The visitors always voice admiration for the teams' collaborative practices, which validates the work of the teachers and reminds them of their accomplishments.

Conclusion

Working collaboratively with colleagues is the second big idea of a PLC. Collaborative teams have been called the engine that drives the PLC process (DuFour et al., 2024). This chapter illustrated how school leaders and systems can celebrate the qualities of high-functioning collaborative teams in a PLC. By using the monitoring tools in this chapter, leaders and teams can measure their success against the indicators of high-functioning collaborative teams, which leads the way to celebrating these teams.

Use the reflection questions (page 107) to reflect on your collaborative team success criteria, your current reality, and how your use of celebration can be strengthened. In the journal prompt questions (page 109), reflect on your personal views about celebrating your collaborative teams. In the next chapter, we examine turning results into celebrations.

Chapter 5 Reflection Questions

Reflect on the following questions from an organizational viewpoint.

1. How would you define a high-functioning collaborative team?

2. What success criteria would your list include for collaborative teams?

3. What is your current reality in establishing and implementing high-functioning collaborative teams?

4. What processes of your collaborative teams can you currently celebrate?

5. What processes of your collaborative teams do you need to strengthen through celebration?

6. Who needs to provide feedback or suggestions on how to celebrate your collaborative teams?

7. Identify the most appropriate time and place to celebrate a high-functioning collaborative team.

Chapter 5 Journal Prompts

Reflect on these questions from a personal viewpoint.

1. How can you increase your understanding of success criteria for collaborative teams?

2. How can you become more actively engaged in your team or school's collaboration process?

3. In your role, how have you celebrated your team's success in meeting success criteria of a high-functioning collaborative team?

Celebrating in a PLC at Work® © 2025 Solution Tree Press • SolutionTree.com
Visit **go.SolutionTree.com/PLCbooks** to download this free reproducible.

You don't get results by focusing on results. You get results by focusing on the actions that produce results.

—**Mike Hawkins**

CHAPTER 6

Celebrating Results

Throughout this book, the focus of the celebrations has been a result of a change in actions. The PLC culture shift is action oriented, and therefore our celebrations are centered on actions that provide the best results. As mentioned in chapter 3 (page 55), collective teacher efficacy has one of the highest impacts on student achievement. However, the intentionality of empowering teachers to know they are making a difference in student learning by giving them the power to collectively make instructional decisions is not enough to sustain the PLC culture shift. As John Hattie remarks in an interview with James Nottingham (The Learning Pit, 2018), "When you fundamentally believe you're making a difference and then you feed it with evidence you are, that is dramatically powerful." The evidence that feeds the belief is the purpose for celebrating the actions and being results oriented. The results are required to turn the belief we are making a positive difference into the confidence we are making a positive difference.

To illustrate this concept, think of a common actionable plan many of us have labored with over the years: losing weight. Maybe you have tried one of these recommended diets by the American Heart Association: the Dietary Approaches to Stop Hypertension (DASH) diet; the Mediterranean, pescatarian, or vegan diet; the Therapeutic Lifestyle Changes (TLC) plan; the South Beach diet; or the Paleolithic diet. There is a good chance you began the diet with some research, preparation, and optimism. Your chosen diet plan had worked for many others before you, and there was no reason it wouldn't work to help you lose weight as well. You faithfully followed the requirements and sacrificed all the joy of eating the delicious foods that led to the need to change the culture of your eating habits. After two or three weeks of losing weight and seeing the results of your new eating habits, you were energized and committed to being faithful to your new actions. However, if after two or three weeks you were not losing weight and not seeing the results of your new eating habits, you would most likely abandon the well-intended diet for a new plan.

Empowering Change Through Results

Members of a PLC realize that all of their efforts in these areas (a focus on learning, collaborative teams, collective inquiry, action orientation, and continuous improvement) must be assessed based on results rather than intentions (DuFour et al., 2024). Since any change in a school's culture will likely require additional work and stress on the instructional staff, evidence of success is necessary to show the collective actions of the collaborative teams are improving learning for all students. Without this evidence, many of the instructional staff will abandon the required changes in the culture shift and return to the practices they have already developed and refined in their classrooms (Goodson, Moore, & Hargreaves, 2006). The celebrated evidence of improvement, whether formative or summative, provides the stimulus to continue building the collective efficacy and responsibility in the new instructional practices. Through acknowledging and celebrating successful new actions, the collaborative team and school staff foster a positive and motivating culture toward growth that stimulates the collective progress toward a change in practices. The sharing, reflecting, and celebrating successful outcomes support the collective efficacy and responsibility to drive the PLC culture shift through collaborative teammates and school administrators collectively celebrating improvements in adult practices and student achievement. This acknowledgment cultivates a sense of unity and shared purpose within the collaborative team, provides evidence of best practices for other collaborative teams, serves as motivation for the doubters, and leaves the resistors with a lack of credibility.

In "Professional Learning With Staying Power," Thomas R. Guskey (2021) states effective professional development encompasses mechanisms for instructional leaders to regularly receive precise feedback regarding the success of their practices. It is not enough for data around the impact of teams' work to exist; it is critical for educators to *see* the implemented changes have created a positive impact on the work of their students. Too often, teachers and administrators are asked to implement a program or initiative without enough training, monitoring, or efficacy in the new practices. The instructional staff puts forth additional energy and time to incorporate, to the best of their ability, what is expected only to find the results were not as advertised. Therefore, it is understandable for some instructional staff to be skeptical of any new changes in current practice. However, when there is an intentional administrative effort in training, monitoring, and building collective efficacy, the final piece to solidify the culture shift is to recognize and celebrate the evidence that their efforts yielded better performance in their students' essential learning. Through this process, teachers gain confidence and efficacy in the new practices and are likely to continue using the practices and seeking other new practices.

According to Guskey (2007), it is critical that the evidence for celebration is based on information from data teachers trust. For this reason, it is important to have a subcommittee focused on results. As mentioned in chapter 3 (page 55), subcommittees are part of your district or school's guiding coalition. It is through the subcommittee work the guiding collation and school staff build their shared knowledge of the PLC process and identify and eliminate barriers to student learning. The work of the results subcommittee focuses on best practices to collect data to drive decisions and what data are credible in driving the decision-making process. The collective inquiry, based on the teacher's perspective of what are credible results, not only builds the collective teacher efficacy and responsibility in the process, but it also validates the results that will be most convincing to teachers that the new practices are making a difference in all students learning at higher levels.

To maximize the collective teacher efficacy and responsibility, build progress-monitoring steps, and identify effective data to celebrate, consensus on what effectiveness looks like needs to occur before the collection of information from data. Before any consideration of a change in policies or practices, teachers need time to address questions such as these (Guskey, 2014): How will we know if this works? What changes in students would we expect to see? What evidence do we trust to show that this innovation makes a positive difference? When instructional leaders determine and plan for the results that matter most as evidence of success, they are more likely to embrace and use the results to drive change in practices (Guskey, 2021). Led by the results subcommittee, this is the responsibility of the guiding coalition to clearly articulate to the staff what success looks like and what will be celebrated publicly and continuously. The guiding coalition must establish new practices with a plan to celebrate evidence of positive effects to ensure teachers embrace new practices proven to be successful based on what teachers determine to be most convincing (Guskey, 2020).

As Guskey (2021) states, educational leaders must progress monitor practices early in the change process and be prepared to acknowledge both successes and struggles. They need to bring instructional leaders together after trying out the new practices to share impressions, compare results, and discuss the next steps. Positive results provide the encouragement teachers need to persist in their efforts. Evidence that shows no improvement can be used to pinpoint problems or difficulties where adaptations in implementation strategies may be required.

Use figure 6.1 (page 114) to establish what information from data is most important to show the changes in practice are making a positive impact on teacher and student learning, the appropriate time to monitor the success of the new practice, and the appropriate time to celebrate the success.

In a results-oriented culture, the responsibility for collective teacher efficacy occurs when teachers collectively decide what is valid in determining success and having the information from data to prove it worked. When using the "Results That Matter" worksheet (figure 6.1, page 114), teachers provide what assessments they value as validation the new practices have significance in improving student learning. Establishing the criteria as formative and end-of-unit assessments provides quick results to celebrate improvements or pinpoint issues that can be corrected before teachers feel frustrated in the process. As a PLC leader, information from the worksheet provides the data needed to confidently and quickly show teachers the new practices work and celebrate with staff the positive impact on teaching practices and student learning.

RESULTS THAT MATTER WORKSHEET

Directions: Collectively, as a guiding coalition, establish what assessment information from data is most important to show the changes in practice are making a positive impact on teacher and student learning, the appropriate time to monitor the success of the new practice, and the appropriate time to celebrate the success. Consider at least one formative assessment, one end-of-unit assessment, and one high-stakes summative assessment.

Your District or School Name:	Date:

Formative Assessment

Assessment	Data
Formative assessment name:	**Current status:**
What evidence do we trust to show that this innovation makes a positive difference?	
	Historical trend (positive, negative, or neutral):
Description of the assessment and why it is important:	**Target:**
How will we know if this works?	*What changes in students would we expect to see?*

End-of-Unit Assessment

Assessment	Data
End-of-unit assessment name:	**Current status:**
What evidence do we trust to show that this innovation makes a positive difference?	
	Historical trend (positive, negative, or neutral):
Description of the assessment and why it is important:	**Target:**
How will we know if this works?	*What changes in students would we expect to see?*

High-Stakes Summative Assessment	
Assessment	**Data**
High-stakes summative assessment name: *What evidence do we trust to show that this innovation makes a positive difference?*	**Current status:**
	Historical trend (positive, negative, or neutral):
Description of the assessment and why it is important: *How will we know if this works?*	**Target:** *What changes in students would we expect to see?*
Key Findings	
Formative Assessment	
Formative assessment results:	
Change from previous status:	
Change in trend (positive, negative, or neutral):	
Target (exceeded, met, or did not meet):	

Figure 6.1: "Results that matter" worksheet.

continued →

End-of-Unit Assessment
End-of-unit assessment results:
Change from previous status:
Change in trend (positive, negative, or neutral):
Target (exceeded, met, or did not meet):
High-Stakes Summative Assessment
High-stakes summative assessment results:
Change from previous status:
Change in trend (positive, negative, or neutral):
Target (exceeded, met, or did not meet):

Recommendations	Celebrations
Formative Assessment	
Formative assessment recommendation:	**Formative assessment action:**
Brief description of the recommendation and its rationale	*Brief description of the action to be taken and responsible person or team*
	Deadline:
	Specific deadline for completion
End-of-Unit Assessment	
End-of-unit assessment recommendation:	**End-of-unit assessment action:**
Brief description of the recommendation and its rationale	*Brief description of the action to be taken and responsible person or team*
	Deadline:
	Specific deadline for completion
High-Stakes Summative Assessment	
High-stakes summative assessment recommendation:	**High-stakes summative assessment action:**
Brief description of the recommendation and it rationale	*Brief description of the action to be taken and responsible person or team*
	Deadline:
	Specific deadline for completion

*Visit **go.SolutionTree.com/PLCbooks** for a free reproducible version of this figure.*

In *Leaders of Learning*, DuFour and Marzano (2011) describe what it means to be results oriented.

1. Instructional leaders must be focused on student results.
2. Everyone works collaboratively toward SMART goals.
3. Everyone collaboratively gathers and analyzes student evidence to inform individual and collective instructional practices.
4. Evidence of student learning is regularly used to identify the specific needs of individual students.
5. Every policy, procedure, program, and practice is assessed based on its impact on student learning.

Using these five commitments to drive our results orientation, we will now look at practical ways districts and schools can recognize and celebrate more teachers and students winning and achieving a personal best during the PLC culture shift.

Turning Results Into Celebrations

In chapter 1 (page 11), we discussed what district leaders, school leaders, and the guiding coalitions consider tight or non-negotiable in the PLC culture shift (DuFour et al., 2024). Collaborative teams will:

1. Work together with collective responsibility for student learning
2. Provide a guaranteed and viable curriculum for all students
3. Use common formative assessments to monitor student learning
4. Use common assessment data to improve teaching and learning practices
5. Provide systematic interventions and extensions for all students

It is these five foundational pieces of the PLC process connected to the five results-oriented commitments from DuFour and Marzano (2011) that drive the collective celebrations to show the new practices are working to improve student learning for all students.

Team Results-Oriented Commitments and Celebrations

Figure 6.1 (page 114) provides an opportunity for your guiding coalition to establish the actions teachers feel are most important to demonstrate the change in practices that are having the desired effect. To focus on maximizing the collective teacher efficacy and responsibility in the PLC process, it is important to remember these actions may be unique to each school district and each school. The actions should be tied to best practices in the field of education; however, this work should not be decided by district or school administrators. These actions are owned by the guiding coalition or collaborative teams of each school. These are the loose celebrations in our results-oriented focus toward actions to drive the PLC culture shift. In *Cultures Built to Last: Systemic PLCs at Work*, Richard DuFour and Michael Fullan (2013) remind leaders to be loose or empower others to make decisions when developing instructional practices. These are the practices related to how the collective group decides to improve learning for all students within the PLC framework of what is tight or nondiscretionary. These loose celebrations are the key to building collective teacher efficacy and responsibility while driving the school culture toward better practices to improve teacher and student learning.

In chapter 3 (page 55), we discussed the need for leaders to be a *host* and not a *hero* to navigate the intricacies as effective leaders in the PLC process. However, there are instances where the superintendent, principal, or other district or school leader must be tight in five foundational areas to ensure learning occurs for all students. Use figure 6.2 to establish the parameters around the actions that are nondiscretionary. This tool will help you create the tight expectations for what all teachers and collaborative teams are expected to accomplish while staying loose with the success criteria as the evidence of accomplishing what is tight in the PLC culture shift.

TURNING RESULTS INTO CELEBRATION	
Directions: Clarity precedes competence, so it's important to clearly define the parameters and expectations around the actions that are tight or nondiscretionary in a PLC culture. Collectively as a guiding coalition create the success criteria as parameters and expectations for what all teachers and collaborative teams are expected to produce as evidence of the tight practices in the PLC culture shift. Designate at least three progress-monitoring and celebration dates throughout the school year to celebrate collaborative teams who have evidence of meeting the expectation.	
Your District or School Name:	Date:
What Is Tight in the PLC Process	Success Criteria, Progress Monitoring and Celebrations
Collaborative teams will work together with collective responsibility for student learning.	
Description of the expectations and why it is important:	Success criteria after year one:
Current reality:	
One-year expectation:	Progress-monitoring and celebration dates:
	Date 1:
	Date 2:
	Date 3:
Provide a guaranteed and viable curriculum for all students.	
Description of the expectations and why it is important:	Success criteria after year one:
Current reality:	
One-year expectation:	Progress-monitoring and celebration dates:
	Date 1:
	Date 2:
	Date 3:

Figure 6.2: Turning results into celebration.

continued →

Use common formative assessments to monitor student learning.	
Description of the expectations and why it is important:	**Success criteria after year one:**
Current reality:	
One-year expectation:	**Progress-monitoring and celebration dates:**
	Date 1:
	Date 2:
	Date 3:

Use common assessment data to improve teaching and learning practices.	
Description of the expectations and why it is important:	**Success criteria after year one:**
Current reality:	
One-year expectation:	**Progress-monitoring and celebration dates:**
	Date 1:
	Date 2:
	Date 3:

Provide systematic interventions and extensions for all students.	
Description of the expectations and why it is important:	**Success criteria after year one:**
Current reality:	

One-year expectation:	Progress-monitoring and celebration dates:		
	Date 1:		
	Date 2:		
	Date 3:		

Visit **go.SolutionTree.com/PLCbooks** *for a free reproducible version of this figure.*

Designate at least three progress-monitoring and celebration dates throughout the school year to celebrate collaborative teams who have evidence of meeting the expectations. Outwardly celebrate collaborative teams after each of the designated days. The teams celebrated after the first date will show other teams the work can be accomplished and serve as role models for collaborative teams still working toward implementation. The second progress-monitoring and celebration date will celebrate teams who overcame obstacles and persevered to improve the foundations of a PLC, and finally, the third date is a celebration of the resiliency of the teacher teams to embrace a collaborative culture. As a leader in the PLC process, you'll use figure 6.2 as a monitoring tool throughout the year. Using the success criteria as a guide, trends and patterns emerge where the collaborative teams struggle and provide you and the guiding coalition data to implement the professional learning necessary to minimize the frustration and positively support the improvement of each collaborative team.

Figure 6.3 (page 122) shows an example of a school system using figure 6.2 to establish an implementation timeline to solidify the five tight foundations of the PLC culture with defined teacher success criteria and progress-monitoring dates to celebrate the collaborative teams *acting* their way into a new way of thinking. Aligning what is tight in a PLC with the results-oriented commitments provides clarity to everyone what actions are valued, examples of evidence during progress monitoring, and what will be the focus of district and school celebrations in the third big idea of being results oriented. Using this document, the district and school guiding coalitions were able to monitor the progress of each collaborative team and celebrate with the school staff and at school board meetings when collaborative teams had evidence new practices were positively impacting student achievement. This document provided collaborative teams clarity in the tight foundations of the PLC culture, an understanding of why the work was critical to improving teaching and learning practices, examples of what the work would look like through the success criteria, and a timeline to show it was a process to implement throughout the school year.

TURNING RESULTS INTO CELEBRATION

Directions: Clarity precedes competence, so it's important to clearly define the parameters and expectations around the actions that are tight or nondiscretionary in a PLC culture. Collectively as a guiding coalition create the success criteria as parameters and expectations for what all teachers and collaborative teams are expected to produce as evidence of the tight practices in the PLC culture shift. Designate at least three progress-monitoring and celebration dates throughout the school year to celebrate collaborative teams who have evidence of meeting the expectation.

Your District or School Name:	Date:

What Is Tight in the PLC Process	Success Criteria, Progress Monitoring and Celebrations

Collaborative teams will work together with collective responsibility for student learning.

Description of the expectations and why it is important:	Success criteria after year one:
To create a culture where teachers and support staff work together to solve problems and learn from one another while assuming responsibility for all students learning on or above grade level in the essential standards. Teachers will be engaged in team collaboration, focused on student data and instruction, for two days per week for forty-five minutes a day.	We have agendas and create minutes for each meeting. We follow norms and accountability steps. We take responsibility for all students. We include support staff in collaboration as appropriate. We analyze end-of-unit data by learning target to determine which students need intervention or extension and which instructional strategies were most successful. We designate team members responsible for intervention or extension based on data. We use the idea of our students, not my students. We are transparent about results. We are open to changing strategies based on data. We trust each other throughout the collaboration process.
Current reality:	
Teachers have been assigned to collaborative teams that have meaning based on the same grade, course, or skills. Most collaborative teams have not established any of the above expectations.	

One-year expectation:	Progress-monitoring and celebration dates:	
All collaborative teams have implemented the Getting Started criteria and have evidence of progress in what is expected all collaborative teams will know and be able to do as a high-functioning team.	Date 1:	October 15
	Date 2:	February 15
	Date 3:	May 15

Provide a guaranteed and viable curriculum for all students.

Description of the expectations and why it is important:	Success criteria after year one:
To create a culture where teachers and support staff work together to determine what is essential for all students to know and be able to do by the end of the grade or course.	We deconstructed all content standards. We used the REAL template. We collaborated vertically by feeder pattern. We can articulate and justify our essential standards. We identified prerequisites in learning progressions and determined proficiency.

Current reality:	
No collaborative teams have identified what is essential for all students to know and be able to do by the end of the grade or course.	
One-year expectation:	**Progress-monitoring and celebration dates:**
Collaborative teams will use the REAL criteria to determine what is most essential for all students to show proficiency by the end of the school year. The essential learning will not be more than one third of the state standards. • Collaborative teams will create learning targets for students to understand what they are expected to learn. • Collaborative teams will create a unit plan to provide response days after each common formative assessment. • Collaborative teams will determine the proficiency level and hold all students to that expectation.	Date 1: November 10 Date 2: March 15 Date 3: May 15

Use common formative assessments to monitor student learning.

Description of the expectations and why it is important:	Success criteria after year one:
To create a culture where teachers and support staff work together to create common formative assessments to be used to monitor student learning throughout Tier 1 instruction. This is critical to ensure students are getting the needed additional support before the end-of-unit assessment.	We created the end-of-unit assessment first using the backward-design process. We created common formative assessment questions for each learning target based on the end-of-unit assessment. We weighted questions based on DOK level. We created SMART goals aligned with culminating formative assessments.
Current reality:	
Collaborative teams are not using common formative assessments as part of their Tier 1 instruction.	
One-year expectation:	**Progress-monitoring and celebration dates:**
Based off the identified essential standards, collaborative teams will create and administer common formative assessments and provide response days during Tier 1 instruction.	Date 1: November 10 Date 2: March 1 Date 3: May 15

Use common assessment data to improve teaching and learning practices.

Description of the expectations and why it is important:	Success criteria after year one:
To create a culture where teachers and support staff use common formative and end-of-unit assessment data to analyze if specific teaching practices yield better results for student learning. This use of common assessments is critical to ensure teaching practices are being measured on the same level of rigor and validity.	We analyze end-of-unit and common formative assessment data. We analyze Tier 1 instructional practices to determine effectiveness. We discuss necessary changes to pacing, assessments, and instructional strategies.

Source: Bartow County School System. Used with permission.

Figure 6.3: Turning results into celebration in the Bartow County School System.

continued →

Current reality:	
Teachers are not using common assessment data to evaluate the impact of teaching practices on student learning.	
One-year expectation:	**Progress-monitoring and celebration dates:**
Collaborative teams will use a data protocol to bring data to collaboration and utilize questions within the protocol to determine which teaching practices had the greatest impact on student achievement. Teachers will discuss the practices deemed to be most effective for student learning.	Date 1: December 1 Date 2: March 10 Date 3: May 15
Provide systematic interventions and extensions for all students.	
Description of the expectations and why it is important:	**Success criteria after year one:**
To create a culture where teachers and support staff use common end-of-unit assessment data to determine which students demonstrate proficiency on the identified essential standards. Students who do not show proficiency will be provided additional time during the school day to continue working on proficiency. Students who are proficient will be provided extended learning in the essential standard.	We have a minimum of thirty minutes per day built into the master schedule to provide students additional learning time in mathematics and English and reading. We have teachers and support staff trained in how to monitor students attending intervention or extension. We have teachers and support staff trained in how to effectively use the additional time to increase student learning.
Current reality:	
There is no time built into the school bell schedule for intervention and extension.	
One-year expectation:	**Progress-monitoring and celebration dates:**
The guiding coalition will develop a schedule to provide all students with intervention or extension during the school day.	Date 1: October 1 Date 2: January 31 Date 3: March 15

In aligning what is monitored and celebrated in the *tight* PLC foundations with the five results-oriented commitments of DuFour and Marzano (2011), it is important for leaders and teachers in a PLC culture to define the work and how to support and celebrate each other while navigating the results-oriented culture.

District and School Results-Oriented Commitments and Celebrations

An examination of DuFour and Marzano's (2011) results-oriented commitments reveals close alignment with the five PLC foundations previously discussed in this chapter. With the district and school guiding coalitions connecting the expectations throughout their respective areas on ensuring what is *tight* is established to support the work of the collaborative teams in improving teaching practices and proficiency for all students on the guaranteed and viable curriculum, it is also necessary for teachers to examine their work in a results-oriented collaborative culture.

In our work, the collaborative teams who excel in the five results-oriented commitments outlined by DuFour and Marzano see the greatest professional and student academic growth.

Let's take a closer look at each of the results-oriented commitments and what practical indicators define a collaborative team working toward and performing as a high-functioning team.

1. **Instructional leaders must be focused on student results:** We are focused on results by student, by target, and by the essential standard or skill. Results are used to adjust teaching practices during Tier 1 prevention and to provide targeted intervention by learning target or extension of content or skill during Tier 2 support. Instructional leaders are focused on student results by prioritizing and taking action steps to ensure student proficiency on the guaranteed and viable curriculum. Collaboration and instruction are focused to ensure every student acquires the knowledge and skills necessary to be successful in the next course, grade, or skill.

2. **Everyone works collaboratively toward SMART goals:** We have analyzed student achievement and subgroup data (for students with disabilities and English language learners) addressing gaps in performance. SMART goals have been established to improve upon the level of achievement we are working interdependently to attain. As noted in the introduction (page 1), SMART goals are strategic and specific, measurable, attainable, results oriented, and time bound, and they focus on common formative assessments, end-of-unit assessments, and high-stakes testing and data points.

3. **Everyone collaboratively gathers and analyzes student evidence to inform individual and collective instructional practices:** We have evidence of instructional adjustments that led to increased student learning on common formative and common end-of-unit assessments. The adjusted instructional practices were a result of collaborative discussions from information collected from our data protocol.

4. **Evidence of student learning is regularly used to identify specific needs of individual students:** We can show growth using student learning proficiency data from common formative assessments and common end-of-unit assessments implemented through Tier 1 preventions and Tier 2 interventions throughout multiple teaching-assessing cycles.

5. **Every policy, procedure, program, and practice is assessed based on its impact on student learning:** We commit to evaluating all aspects of classroom instructional practices through an ongoing data-driven process to determine their influences on student learning outcomes to promote continuous improvement and accountability in our teaching practices.

Establishing the success criteria for collaborative teams provides the clarity often missing when teacher teams begin the work in a PLC. Use the results-oriented commitments and aligned success criteria in figure 6.4 (page 126) to determine each collaborative team's current reality. When this survey is used quarterly throughout the school year, teacher teams and school leaders can monitor and celebrate when teams have a results orientation embedded in their collaborative culture. It is important to celebrate and share practices with the entire staff when teams score 22 or higher on the survey. These teams have results orientation embedded in their collaborative culture and will serve as role models for other teams who may be struggling to integrate the focus on results.

RESULTS-ORIENTED SUCCESS CRITERIA: PROGRESS-MONITORING AND CELEBRATION SURVEY		
1 = Not Evident; 3 = In Progress; 5 = Embedded in Our Culture		
Indicator	Success Criteria	Rating
We are focused on results by student, by target, and by the essential standard or skill. Results are used to adjust teaching practices during Tier 1 prevention and to provide targeted intervention by learning target or extension of content or skill during Tier 2 support.	We have clear and measurable assessments for students aligned by learning target and designed to promote student growth and proficiency in the essential standards or skills.	1
	We monitor the progress of students and hold each other accountable in facilitating student learning.	3
	We ensure that all students, regardless of their background, have equal access to the essential standards or skills.	
	We hold ourselves accountable for the academic success of all students in the identified essential standards or skills.	5
We have analyzed student achievement and subgroup data, addressing gaps in performance. SMART goals have been established to improve upon the level of achievement we are working interdependently to attain. SMART goals focus on common formative assessments, end-of-unit assessments, and high-stakes assessments and data points.	We establish Tier 1 prevention and Tier 2 intervention and extension SMART goals by essential learning unit.	1
	We establish long-term SMART goals using previous year's data (MAP, Milestones, common summative assessments).	
	We can articulate how SMART goals support the school and district goals.	3
		5
We have evidence of instructional adjustments that led to increased student learning on common formative and end-of-unit assessments. The adjusted instructional practices were a result of collaborative discussions from information collected from our data protocol.	We analyze common formative assessment and end-of-unit data.	1
	We analyze Tier 1 instruction to determine effectiveness.	
	We discuss necessary changes to pacing, assessments, and instructional strategies.	3
	We examine assessment protocols to determine validity.	
	We analyze effectiveness of our SMART goal after Tier 1 prevention and Tier 2 intervention.	5
We can show growth using student learning proficiency data from common formative assessments and common summative assessments implemented through Tier 1 preventions and Tier 2 interventions throughout multiple teaching-assessing cycles.	We respond to data with targeted preventions and interventions to address misconceptions.	1
	We reassess after Tier 2 intervention to determine effectiveness of interventions, student growth, and proficiency level.	3
		5
We commit to evaluating all aspects of classroom instructional practices through an ongoing data-driven process to determine their influences on student learning outcomes in order to promote continuous improvement and accountability in our teaching practices.	We use data to thoroughly assess every classroom practice and instructional program for its impact on student learning.	1
	We have a system for continuous instructional improvement. If an instructional practice or program is found to have a negative impact on student learning, we revise, refine, or discontinue it in favor of more researched-based practices.	3
	We hold ourselves accountable for the impact of our decisions on student learning and will adjust instructional plans when necessary.	5
Celebrate teams who score 22 or higher as an example of the right work.	Total:	

Figure 6.4: Results-oriented success criteria—Progress-monitoring and celebration survey.

Visit go.SolutionTree.com/PLCbooks for a free reproducible version of this figure.

Celebrating Results Through Tiers of Support

In *Taking Action*, Austin Buffum, Mike Mattos, and Janet Malone (2018) present the RTI at Work pyramid. This inverted pyramid structures the support for student learning into three tiers.

1. **Tier 1 prevention:** Core grade-level essential learning for all students
2. **Tier 2 interventions and extensions:** Additional time and support for students based on their proficiency in the essential learning
3. **Tier 3 reteaching:** Intense reteaching for students who are multiple years below grade level on a universal skill

To ensure instructional staff see the impact of their collective decisions in all three tiers of instructional support impacting student learning on the essential standards and behaviors, staff need to establish, monitor, and celebrate information from data to continue driving their adjustments for student learning. A universally accepted method for writing goals is the SMART goal process (Doran, 1981). Using this method as a model for consistency throughout the district or school allows leadership to monitor actions, progress, and celebrations by the collaborative team, by subject area or grade level, by the school, and by the district. Since Tier 1 prevention directly impacts Tier 2 intervention and extension, we recommend including both tiers in the SMART goal.

Figure 6.5 (page 128) provides a model for collaborative teams, schools, and districts to use in setting goals for Tier 1 prevention and Tier 2 intervention and extension. This systematic process uses the four critical questions to drive the goals and aids in the backward design of essential unit planning, provides subject-area or grade-level and school-performance progress monitoring for the guiding coalition, and collectively allows the school and district support staff to quickly identify gaps in learning and trends of success to be celebrated. It is important to celebrate when the collaborative team has improved in their instructional practices. Using this document provides information from data that must drive the instructional practices used in the classroom to improve student success during both Tier 1 prevention and Tier 2 intervention and extension. It also provides opportunities to celebrate as teammates and with the staff when Tier 1 and Tier 2 proficiency goals are met and there is clear evidence that all students are reaching proficiency on the identified essential standards and skills.

CELEBRATING OUR TEAM'S SUCCESS, THE SMART WAY

Directions: Complete the Tier 1 and Tier 2 goal essential learning name and description sections with the details of your specific goals.

For each SMART criterion, write down your target or the specific details related to that criterion.

The common formative target (%) and performance (%) will be decided by the number of common formative assessments the collaborative team determines.

The overall progress (%) will conclude for Tier 1 after the end-of-unit assessment, and the Tier 2 goal will conclude at the end of the time frame the collaborative team determines for students to continue to work toward proficiency of the essential learning.

Use the comments, suggestions, and celebrations section to indicate any relevant comments or suggestions related to your goal and indicate how you will celebrate student success and teacher success.

Collaborative Team:

Tier 1 Essential Learning

Specific goal description (What is it you want students to know and be able to do?):

Measurable goal description (How will we know if each student has learned it?):

Attainable (What instructional practices will be provided to all students?):

	Target (%)	Performance (%)
CFA 1	_____ (%)	_____ (%)
CFA 2	_____ (%)	_____ (%)
CFA 3	_____ (%)	_____ (%)
End-of-Unit Assessment	_____ (%)	_____ (%)

Realistic assessment results (What percentage of students will be proficient throughout the unit on common formative assessments [CFAs] and on the assessment at the end of the essential learning unit?):

Timely (What is the timeline to meet our goal?):

Start date: _____ **End date:** _____

Total days to demonstrate Tier 1 proficiency: _____

Tier 1 celebrations:

What did we learn from each other during this unit? How did we make each other better?

What did the information from data show we did well to support all students learning on or above grade level?

What did the information from data show we can adjust in our next essential learning unit to improve our Tier 1 proficiency results?

Figure 6.5: Celebrating our team's success the SMART way.

continued →

Tier 2 Essential Learning
Specific goal description (How will we respond when some students do not learn it?):
Specific goal description (How will we extend the learning for students who have demonstrated proficiency?):
Measurable goal description (How will we know if each student has learned it?):
Attainable (What instructional practices will be provided to students in intervention and extension?):

Realistic assessment results (What percentage of students will be proficient at the end of Tier 2 intervention?)		
	Target (%)	Performance (%)
Intervention Reassessment 1	_____ (%)	_____ (%)
Intervention Reassessment 2	_____ (%)	_____ (%)
Intervention Reassessment 3	_____ (%)	_____ (%)
Intervention Reassessment 4	_____ (%)	_____ (%)

Timely (What is the timeline to meet our goal?):

Start date:		End date:	
Total days to demonstrate Tier 1 proficiency:			

Tier 2 celebrations:

What did we learn during intervention to support students needing additional time and support or extension in the essential learning?

What did the information from data show we did well to support all students learning on or above grade level during the additional Tier 2 time frame?

What did the information from data show we can adjust in our next Tier 2 cycle of time to support students reaching proficiency on the essential learning?

Visit **go.SolutionTree.com/PLCbooks** *for a free reproducible version of this figure.*

Celebrating Summative Results

In chapter 1 (page 11), we discussed formative and summative celebrations. Formative celebrations are the small celebrations that occur daily during collaboration meetings, a visit during Tier 1 instruction, or the success of an activity during extension time. The summative celebrations are the schoolwide celebrations recognized in front of the entire staff, posted on social media, and celebrated during a school board meeting. These celebrations may include all collaborative teams who met their essential standard SMART goals, achieved 100 percent student proficiency on the essential standard after Tier 2 interventions, or beat the state average and improved results on a state assessment. As you have seen throughout these chapters, the formative celebrations are the small daily, weekly, or monthly celebrations that provide immediate results showing the new actions or practices are making a positive impact on teacher and student learning. However, celebrating your way through the PLC culture shift will require a celebration of the totality of improved practices and results through your focus on learning, collaboration, and being results oriented.

In the introduction (page 1), we highlighted the highest award a teacher can receive in the Bartow County School System: The High-Functioning Collaborative Team Award. True to the ideals of a PLC, an individual cannot achieve this recognition. A teacher can only be celebrated for this highest achievement as a member of a high-functioning collaborative team who works interdependently to achieve common goals that directly impact student achievement. Members of a high-functioning collaborative team are willing and eager to learn from one another. Team members honor their collective commitments to one another, creating an atmosphere of trust and mutual respect. Violations of the commitments are addressed, and members use them as the basis for crucial conversations and honest dialogue. A team maintains a focus on learning, collaborative culture, and collective responsibility, and remains results oriented. There is evidence that all students are learning at higher levels with Tier 2 intervention for students who were not proficient on the end-of-unit assessment and extension for those students who were proficient.

Figure 6.6 provides the collective work of the Bartow County School System's celebration subcommittee's recommendation in promoting the compilation of actions that encompasses the five PLC tight foundations, the three big ideas, and the four critical questions that drive the work in a PLC. After consensus by the Bartow County School System guiding coalition, the ultimate summative celebration was established with the purpose to recognize and celebrate collaborative teams who embody the best practices that improve teacher and student learning. A celebration is available to every teacher who embraces the role of a collaborative teammate, a commitment to collective inquiry, and the use of common assessment information to make decisions regarding teacher practices and student learning, and who measures their success based on the value of improving the collaborative team and the team's success regarding the proficiency of all students on the identified essential learning—and, of course, gets results.

As you begin or continue your investment in staff and student learning through the PLC process, some teachers and administrators may see the work as too laborious, intrusive, or unattainable. It may seem plausible to improve in some areas but not in all the expectations that

> **A-TEAM APPLICATION**
>
> Thank you for your commitment to becoming a high-functioning collaborative team. The application has four phases.
>
> 1. **Team-level assessment:** The collaborative team uses the high-functioning collaborative team application to rate their performance within the three big ideas. If they score greater than 90 percent, the team then submits the application to their guiding coalition.
> 2. **School-level review:** The local school guiding coalition uses the high-functioning collaborative team application to assess the collaborative team. If the team scores 90 percent or higher, they submit results to the principal.
> 3. **System-level observation:** The system-level team observes and interviews the collaborative team. The collaborative team will receive constructive feedback and possible next steps.
> 4. **Review with the superintendent:** The superintendent interviews the collaborative team. If awarded high-functioning collaborative team status, the team will be celebrated at a board meeting and present at future professional learning.

Source: Bartow County School System. Used with permission.
Figure 6.6: High-Functioning Collaborative Team (A-Team) application.

*Visit **go.SolutionTree.com/PLCbooks** for a free reproducible version of this figure.*

improve teacher and student learning. The high-functioning collaborative team recognition is the evidence of willing and able teachers committed to acting their way into a new way of thinking for the sake of teacher and student learning. Once you celebrate your first high-functioning collaborative team, it will be evident to the entire organization that the PLC process does work with the results to prove it. Before you know it, your one high-functioning collaborative team will turn into a multitude of high-functioning collaborative teams ready to be role models for other teachers and collaborative teams.

Teams that have a cumulative score of 90 percent or above on their self-rating and their local school leadership rating along with relevant evidence connected to the three big ideas (focus on learning, collaboration and collective responsibility, and results orientation) will be considered for review by the system review team. Prior to acceptance for review, a confirmation meeting with leadership is held.

The system review team review includes team collaboration observation, a team interview from the system leadership team, and a thorough review of high-functioning collaborative team evidence of growth in student achievement. Feedback from the system review team will occur within forty-eight hours of the site visit. Dates will be set upon the acceptance of applications from the system leadership team and local school high-functioning collaborative team applicants. The principal will be present during the collaboration observation and high-functioning collaborative team interview.

Use the rating scale in figure 6.7 (page 134), along with the success criteria and possible artifacts for each strand, to indicate the extent to which each statement is true of your collaborative team. Document and attach all relevant data associated with each strand.

HIGH-FUNCTIONING COLLABORATIVE TEAM APPLICATION REVIEW WORKSHEET				
Directions: Use the following rating scale along with the success criteria and possible artifacts for each strand to indicate the extent to which each statement is true of your collaborative team. Document and attach all relevant data associated with each strand.				
1 = Not true of our team; 5 = Our team is getting there; 10 = True of our team				
Core Commitment 1: Focus on Learning				
	Strand		Success Criteria and Artifacts	
1.1	We have worked through the REAL process to properly identify the essential standards for our subject area.			
	Success Criteria	Possible Artifacts	Rating	
	We deconstructed all content standards. We used the REAL template. We collaborated vertically by feeder pattern. We can articulate and justify our essential standards.	REAL templates Milestone weight sheet Standards that are connected from above and below Meeting minutes and agendas Pictures or minutes of vertical alignment Milestone domain data (to know where to focus) MAP projections	1 5 10	
1.2	Appropriate learning targets with learning progressions are identified as key components of the essential standard, and instructional planning is geared to ensure students meet proficiency including preventions, interventions, and reteaching.			
	Success Criteria	Possible Artifacts	Rating	
	We identified success criteria for both teachers and students. We identified prerequisites in learning progressions and determined proficiency. We communicate criteria for success to students, teachers, and parents. Our students self-assess using the learning progression.	Success criteria document Teaching and assessing unit plan (flow chart) Agenda and minutes Common formative (Tier 1) and common summative assessment (Tier 2) data	1 5 10	
1.3	We have outlined the sequencing and pacing for each essential standard and illustrated our prevention, intervention, and reteaching strategies.			
	Success Criteria	Possible Artifacts	Rating	
	We created a sequencing and pacing pencil plan for each essential standard. We reviewed and adjusted based on last year's data. We identified common formative and common summative assessment days. We identified response days for prevention (Tier 1). We discussed achievement by target or standard by student following common formative and common summative assessments. We used data to drive instruction. We obtained outside support for students.	Sequencing and pacing guides Unit plans Master schedule Prevention documentation (Tier 1) Intervention documentation (Tier 2) Reteaching documentation (Tier 3) School pyramid of interventions Communication with stakeholders	1 5 10	

1.4	We have developed our common summative assessments (CSAs) and corresponding common formative assessments (CFAs) establishing appropriate proficiency and DOK levels through data-driven analysis.				
	Success Criteria	**Possible Artifacts**	**Rating**		
	We created the CSA first using a backward-design process. We created questions for each learning target. We used the CSA to develop CFAs. We used evidence-based resources while developing assessments. + GaDOE Resources + Illuminate DNA We weighted questions based on DOK level. We defined proficiency for each CSA and CFA.	CSAs and CFAs Essential standards with corresponding CSA and CFA questions	1	5	10
1.5	The instructional techniques are rigorous research-based strategies fostering high student performance on common summative assessments, MAP, Milestones, and other assessment platforms.				
	Success Criteria	**Possible Artifacts**	**Rating**		
	We used backward design to create rigorous assessments as a blueprint for instruction. We created SMART goals aligned with culminating assessments (Milestones, CTAE Certifications). We used the rigor quadrant to support Hattie's *Visible Learning* effect size.	Detailed teaching-assessing cycle calendar SMART goal documentation and data Unit plans with research-based instructional strategies (appropriate effect size/rigor matrix)	1	5	10
			Subtotal:	____ / 50	
Comments:					

Source: Bartow County School System. Used with permission.

Figure 6.7: High-functioning collaborative team application review worksheet.

continued →

Directions: Use the following rating scale along with the success criteria and possible artifacts for each strand to indicate the extent to which each statement is true of your collaborative team. Document and attach all relevant data associated with each strand.					
1 = Not true of our team; 5 = Our team is getting there; 10 = True of our team					
Core Commitment 2: Collaborative Culture and Collective Responsibility					
Strand		**Success Criteria and Artifacts**			
2.1	We have identified team norms and protocols identifying student learning as a focus to guide us in working collaboratively.				
	Success Criteria	Possible Artifacts	Rating		
	We identified team norms focused on student learning. Norms address the four guiding questions. We identified protocols for norm violations. We review norms at the beginning of each meeting. We review norms and violations periodically and update as needed.	Norms and violations are on agendas. Norms and violations are posted in collaboration area.	1	5	10
2.2	We have established a collegial environment where all members participate and have a connection and understanding of all students we serve. Each member can articulate all aspects of the PLC process.				
	Success Criteria	Possible Artifacts	Rating		
	We trust each other as professionals. We established clear roles. We follow norms and accountability steps. We take responsibility for all students. We plan Tier 1 prevention and Tier 2 interventions. We include support staff in collaboration as appropriate. We are engaged during collaboration. We use correct PLC vocabulary: Tier 1 = Prevention, Tier 2 = Intervention, Tier 3 = Reteaching.	Norms and accountability steps Team roles Data prepared before meeting Agendas and minutes	1	5	10
2.3	Roles and responsibilities have been established where all members have accountability toward student learning. Responsibilities are distributed to team members to address intervention and extension activities, and evidence of those implemented instructional strategies is observable.				
	Success Criteria	Possible Artifacts	Rating		
	We analyze common summative assessment data by learning target to determine. + Which students need intervention or extension? + Which instructional strategies were most successful? We designate team members responsible for intervention or extension based on data.	Collaborative team agendas and minutes Intervention plans	1	5	10

2.4	We have a pervasive culture of collaboratively evaluating student work, sharing effective instructional strategies, sharing what strategies did not work, and assessing prerequisite skills.				
	Success Criteria	**Possible Artifacts**	**Rating**		
	We use the idea of our students, not my students. We score common summative and common formative assessments collaboratively. We are transparent about results. We are open to changing strategies based on data. We trust each other throughout the collaboration process. We share students during Tier 2 intervention. We document strategies being used to drive reflection. We start and end the process with fidelity.	Common formative and summative assessment protocol form Learning targets Grade-level minutes Collaboration logs Reflection standards Collaboration agendas	1	5	10
2.5	When facing an obstacle of learning, collaboration, and results unique to our team, we develop strategies and processes to overcome the barriers.				
	Success Criteria	**Possible Artifacts**	**Rating**		
	We can discuss or provide written commentary displaying our instructional agility. We have a norm addressing barriers. We use support staff when barriers arise.	Collaborative team agendas Written commentary Pencil plans Lesson plans or modified assessments to show examples of experimentation Modified schedules addressing barriers	1	5	10
			Subtotal:	____ / 50	
Comments:					

continued →

Directions: Use the following rating scale along with the success criteria and possible artifacts for each strand to indicate the extent to which each statement is true of your collaborative team. Document and attach all relevant data associated with each strand.

1 = Not true of our team; 5 = Our team is getting there; 10 = True of our team

Core Commitment 3: Results Orientation

Strand	Success Criteria and Artifacts				
3.1	We have analyzed student achievement and subgroup data (SWD and ESOL) addressing gaps in performance. SMART goals have been established to improve upon the level of achievement we are working interdependently to attain.				
	Success Criteria	**Possible Artifacts**	**Rating**		
	We establish long-term SMART goals using previous year's data (MAP, Milestones, common summative assessments). We establish short-term SMART goals to progress monitor our long-term SMART goals. We can articulate how SMART goals support the school and district goal.	SMART goals written and posted Unit plans Data protocols Tier 2 data form	1	5	10
3.2	We can show growth using student learning proficiency data from common formative assessments and common summative assessments implemented through Tier 1 preventions and Tier 2 interventions throughout multiple teaching-assessing cycles.				
	Success Criteria	**Possible Artifacts**	**Rating**		
	We respond to data with targeted preventions and interventions to address misconceptions. We reassess after Tier 2 to determine: + Effectiveness of interventions + Student growth + Proficiency level	Data tracker (protocol) Assessments	1	5	10
3.3	We have evidence of instructional adjustments that led to increased student learning on common formative assessments (CFAs) and common summative assessments (CSAs).				
	Success Criteria	**Possible Artifacts**	**Rating**		
	We analyze CFA and CSA data. We analyze Tier 1 instruction to determine effectiveness. We discuss necessary changes to pacing, assessments, and instructional strategies. We examine assessment protocols to determine validity. We continually revisit pencil pacing guides to adjust instruction. We analyze effectiveness of our SMART goal after Tier 1 prevention and Tier 2 intervention.	Collaborative team data sheets Tier 2 data CFA protocol CSA documentation Updated pacing guides and unit plans	1	5	10

3.4	Our students play an active role in setting their learning goals and monitoring their results.				
	Success Criteria	**Possible Artifacts**	**Rating**		
	Our students invest in their learning by setting their own goals. Our students monitor their progress using their learning progressions as a tool. We write intentional comments on progress reports. We determine Tier 2 interventions to guarantee proficiency and above. We facilitate student-led parent-teacher conferences.	Learning progressions Goal sheets and reflection statements Student self-assessment forms Student progress chart posted in room Common formative and summative assessment data log Progress reports Student data notebooks	1	5	10
3.5	We calibrate how we assess evidence of student learning while aligning rigor levels to district and state assessments.				
	Success Criteria	**Possible Artifacts**	**Rating**		
	We collaborate with support staff to ensure consistent expectations. We establish success criteria for students prior to beginning the unit. We use the blueprint or rigor matrix to align rigor levels to district, state, and outside testing.	Unit plan GMAS blueprint Rigor matrix	1	5	10
			Subtotal:	____ / 50	
Comments:					

Visit **go.SolutionTree.com/PLCbooks** *for a free reproducible version of this figure.*

The beginning of the high-functioning collaborative team application outlines the progress monitoring, collection of evidence, and interviews required to be recognized as a high-functioning collaborative team. The collaborative team should unpack the application for clarity and begin the process using the application to rate their performance with the three big ideas of the PLC process. If they score greater than 90 percent, the team then submits the application to their guiding coalition. The school guiding coalition uses the A-Team application to assess the collaborative team. If the team scores 90 percent or higher, they submit results to the system-level team. If the school guiding coalition does not score the team at 90 percent or higher, specific feedback and professional learning are provided to improve the areas of weakness. Once 90 percent is achieved by the collaborative team, a system-level team observes and interviews the collaborative team. This is a critical step where teams are provided more intentional professional learning from the district's academic support team to become high-functioning collaborative team ready, or they are recommended to the superintendent or the superintendent's designee for the final interview. If, after the final interview, the collaborative team is awarded high-functioning collaborative team status, the team will be celebrated at a board meeting and lead a breakout session at the new teacher institute and other district-led professional learning events.

Conclusion

Throughout this book, we have advocated for celebration as both a recognition of success and a catalyst for continued success. Celebrating results is to celebrate changes in action—changes in the right work that teams within PLCs do to shift the culture of a school. This chapter focused on turning results into celebrations at both the team and the school and district levels—through celebrating results within the three tiers of RTI (formative results—small wins) and celebrating the highest wins (summative results) with the High-Functioning Collaborative Team Award.

Use the reflection questions to reflect on how your school or district celebrates results and how this action would change your school or district culture. In the journal prompt questions (page 142), reflect on your personal views about results-oriented celebration.

Chapter 6 Reflection Questions

Reflect on these questions from an organizational viewpoint.

1. In what ways does the district or school currently measure and track results? Are these measures aligned with what teachers believe are most important to measure learning for all students?

2. How does your district, school, or collaborative team celebrate learning from each other?

3. Which celebration tools in this chapter could have the most immediate impact on the instructional staff to encourage a change in teacher behaviors?

4. How could a celebration plan focused on recognizing and celebrating the success of collective results of the collaborative team change the school culture?

5. How would teachers in your district or school embrace an A-Team recognition and celebration to demonstrate success in the PLC culture?

Chapter 6 Journal Prompts

Reflect on these questions from a personal viewpoint.

1. What, if any, concerns do you have with measuring your effectiveness on learning directly to identified results?

2. How can a results-oriented focus improve your ability to collaborate effectively with others?

3. What concerns, if any, do you have regarding a celebration plan focused only on the success of the collaborative team?

4. What excites you about a celebration plan focused on recognizing and celebrating the success of the collaborative team?

Epilogue

As the high-functioning collaborative team we first met in the introduction to this book finished their presentation to applause and a standing ovation at the board meeting celebration, the superintendent invited board members to the floor to recognize each team member and their principal. The teachers each received a personalized certificate of recognition, and the principal received a plaque honoring the work of the local school guiding coalition in providing the leadership for the teacher team. As a final recognition of their accomplishment, each member was presented with a quarter-zip pullover with an embroidered emblem identifying them as a recognized high-functioning collaborative team. Pictures were taken for social media and the newspaper. Hugs and handshakes with each board member concluded the evening celebration.

The school board recognition is the culmination of teachers embracing the culture of a PLC. It is a showcase of teachers building shared knowledge and collective inquiry around best practices impacting student achievement. It is the tale of resiliency through a culture shift that did not always make sense or come easy. In many cases, it is a celebration of the small victories over the course of multiple years of leaning on each other for support and progress. The night honors the collaborative team members who confidently stood before the superintendent, school board members, their school guiding coalition, family, and friends to tell their story of success within a PLC. Each story is different: a different barrier to overcome, a different peer relationship to strengthen, and a different personal mindset to change. However, each team had to collectively focus on achieving and thriving within the culture shifts of a PLC at Work.

For the superintendent, each team recognition is the confirmation of the value the school board saw in a new way forward through PLCs, validation of the collective inquiry and efficacy of the district guiding coalition's leadership, and admiration for the teachers and support staff who committed to a PLC process. With each team recognition in the Bartow County School System, there is another role model for teachers to connect with for support, an example for new teachers of what is expected when you work in the system, a team of teachers who honor one another through their collective commitments, a class roster of students who are ready for their next grade or subject, and a community recognizing a positive and powerful shift in their schools through the collective work of district and school staff members.

As this work unfolds in schools around the world each day, we need to remember the true purpose of a PLC: educators working collaboratively in ongoing processes of collective inquiry and action research to achieve better results for the students they serve with the assumption that the key to improving learning for students is continuous, job-embedded learning for educators (DuFour et al., 2024). We must never forget this work is about us, the educators, but for them, the students.

References and Resources

Ainsworth, L. (2015, February 24). Priority standards: The power of focus. *Education Week*. Accessed at www.edweek.org/teaching-learning/opinion-priority-standards-the-power-of-focus/2015/02 on June 20, 2024.

Amabile, T. M., & Kramer, S. J. (2011). *The progress principle: Using small wins to ignite joy, engagement, and creativity at work*. Boston: Harvard Business Review Press.

Bailey, K., & Jakicic, C. (2023). *Common formative assessment: A toolkit for Professional Learning Communities at Work* (2nd ed.). Bloomington, IN: Solution Tree Press.

Bartow County School System. (2023). *Bartow County School System Professional Learning Communities Play* (4th ed.). Cartersville, GA: Bartow County School System.

Blackburn, B. R. (2008). *Rigor is not a four-letter word*. Larchmont, NY: Eye on Education.

Buckingham, M. (2005). *The one thing you need to know: About great managing, great leading, and sustained individual success*. New York: Free Press.

Buffum, A., & Mattos, M. (2020). *RTI at Work plan book*. Bloomington, IN: Solution Tree Press.

Buffum, A., Mattos, M, & Malone, J. (2018). *Taking action: A handbook for RTI at Work*. Bloomington, IN: Solution Tree Press.

David, J. L. (2008). What research says about . . ./Pacing guides. *Educational Leadership*, *66*(2). Accessed at https://ascd.org/el/articles/pacing-guides on June 15, 2024.

Dimich, N. (2014). *Design in five: Essential phases to create engaging assessment practice*. Bloomington, IN: Solution Tree Press.

Donohoo, J., Hattie, J., & Eells, R. (2018). The power of collective efficacy. *Educational Leadership, 75*(6). Accessed at https://ascd.org/el/articles/the-power-of-collective-efficacy on July 23, 2024.

Doran, G. T. (1981). There's a S.M.A.R.T. way to write management's goals and objectives. *Management Review, 70*(11), 35–36.

DuFour, R. [Rebecca DuFour]. (n.d.). *The foundation of a PLC* [Video]. Solution Tree Global PD Teams. Accessed at https://app.globalpd.com/search/content/NTQ= on June 15, 2024.

DuFour, R. (2004). What is a "professional learning community"? *Educational Leadership, 61*(8), 6–11. Accessed at www.siprep.org/uploaded/ProfessionalDevelopment/Readings/PLC.pdf on June 15, 2024.

DuFour, R. (2015). *In praise of American educators: And how they can become even better*. Bloomington, IN: Solution Tree Press.

DuFour, R., DuFour, R., & Eaker, R. (2008). *Revisiting Professional Learning Communities at Work: New insights for improving schools*. Bloomington, IN: Solution Tree Press.

DuFour, R., DuFour, R., Eaker, R., & Many, T. W. (2010). *Collaborative teams in Professional Learning Communities at Work: Learning by doing*. Bloomington, IN: Solution Tree Press.

DuFour, R., DuFour, R., Eaker, R., Many, T. W., Mattos, M., & Muhammad, A. (2024). *Learning by doing: A handbook for Professional Learning Communities at Work* (4th ed.). Bloomington, IN: Solution Tree Press.

DuFour, R., DuFour, R., Eaker, R., Mattos, M., & Muhammad, A. (2021). *Revisiting Professional Learning Communities at Work: Proven insights for sustained, substantive school improvement* (2nd ed.). Bloomington, IN: Solution Tree Press.

DuFour, R., & Fullan, M. (2013). *Cultures built to last: Systemic PLCs at Work*. Bloomington IN: Solution Tree Press.

DuFour, R., & Marzano, R. (2011). *Leaders of learning: How district, school, and classroom leaders improve student achievement*. Bloomington, IN: Solution Tree Press.

Eaker, R., Hagadone, M., Keating, J., & Rhoades, M. (2021). *Leading PLCs at Work districtwide: From boardroom to classroom*. Bloomington IN: Solution Tree Press.

Eaker, R., & Keating, J. (2008, Summer). A shift in school culture. *Journal of Staff Development, 29*(3), 14–17. Accessed at https://learningforward.org/wp-content/uploads/2008/06/A-Shift-In-School-Culture.pdf on June 15, 2024.

Erkens, C. (2014a, May 17). *Three reasons your team needs common summative assessments* [Blog post]. Accessed at www.allthingsplc.info/blog/view/251/three-reasons-your-team-needs-common-summative-assessments on July 23, 2024.

Erkens, C. (2014b, November 20). *The power of confusion* [Blog post]. Accessed at www.solutiontree.com/blog/the-power-of-confusion on June 20, 2024.

Erkens, C., Schimmer, T., & Dimich, N. (2018). *Instructional agility: Responding to assessment with real-time decisions*. Bloomington, IN: Solution Tree Press.

Fisher, D., & Frey, N. (2015). *Unstoppable learning: Seven essential elements to unleash student potential*. Bloomington, IN: Solution Tree Press.

Goodson, I., Moore, S., & Hargreaves, A. (2006). Teacher nostalgia and the sustainability of reform: The generation and degeneration of teachers' missions, memory, and meaning. *Educational Administration Quarterly, 42*(1), 42–61.

Graham, P., & Ferriter, W. M. (2010). *Building a Professional Learning Community at Work: A guide to the first year.* Bloomington, IN: Solution Tree Press.

Guskey, T. R. (2007). Multiple sources of evidence: An analysis of stakeholders' perceptions of various indicators of student learning. *Educational Measurement: Issues and Practice, 26*(1), 19–27.

Guskey, T. R. (2014). Planning professional learning. *Educational Leadership, 71*(8), 10–16.

Guskey, T. R. (2020). Flip the script on change. *The Learning Professional, 41*(2), 18–22.

Guskey, T. R. (2021). Professional learning with staying power. *Educational Leadership, 78*(5), 54–59.

Hall, B. (2022). *Powerful guiding coalitions: How to build and sustain the leadership team in your PLC at Work.* Bloomington, IN: Solution Tree Press.

Hattie, J. A. C. (2009). *Visible Learning: A synthesis of over 800 meta-analyses relating to achievement.* London: Routledge.

Hattie, J. A. C. (2012). *Visible learning for teachers: Maximizing impact on learning.* New York: Routledge.

Hersey, P. H., Blanchard, K. H., & Johnson, D. E. (2013). *Management of organizational behavior: Leading human resources* (10th ed.). Boston: Pearson.

Hoover, G. (2020). *The three greatest American companies of all time.* Accessed at https://americanbusinesshistory.org/the-three-greatest-american-companies-of-all-time on June 20, 2024.

Jotkoff, E. (2022, February 1). *NEA survey: Massive staff shortages in schools leading to educator burnout; alarming number of educators indicating they plan to leave profession* [Press release]. Accessed at www.nea.org/about-nea/media-center/press-releases/nea-survey-massive-staff-shortages-schools-leading-educator-burnout-alarming-number-educators on June 23, 2024.

Kolzow, D. R. (2014). *Leading from within: Building organizational leadership capacity.* Accessed at www.iedconline.org/clientuploads/Downloads/edrp/Leading_from_Within.pdf on August 11, 2024.

Kotter, J. P. (2012). *Leading change.* Boston: Harvard Business Review Press.

The Learning Pit. (2018, May 1). *Hattie: Collective efficacy* [Video]. Vimeo. Accessed at https://vimeo.com/267382804 on July 23, 2024.

Many, T. W., Maffoni, M. J., Sparks, S. K., & Thomas, T. F. (2020). *How schools thrive: Building a coaching culture for collaborative teams in PLCs at Work.* Bloomington IN: Solution Tree Press.

Many, T. W., & Sparks-Many, S. K. (2014). *Leverage: Using PLCs to promote lasting improvement in schools.* Thousand Oaks, CA: Corwin.

Marzano, R. J. (2019). *The handbook for the new art and science of teaching.* Bloomington, IN: Solution Tree Press.

Mattos, M. (2015). *Are we a group or a team? Moving from coordination to collaboration in a PLC at Work.* Bloomington, IN: Solution Tree Press.

Meacham, M. (2021, December 14). *Why journaling is a useful learning tool* [Blog post]. Accessed at www.td.org/atd-blog/why-journaling-is-a-useful-learning-tool on June 15, 2024.

Moll T., Jordet G., & Pepping G. (2010). Emotional contagion in soccer penalty shootouts: Celebration of individual success is associated with ultimate team success. *Journal of Sports Science. 28*, 983–992.

Muhammad, A. (2018). *Transforming school culture: How to overcome staff division* (2nd ed.). Bloomington, IN: Solution Tree Press.

National Center for Education Statistics. (2022). *Mathematics and reading scores of fourth- and eighth-graders declined in most states during pandemic, Nation's Report Card shows.* Accessed at www.prnewswire.com/news-releases/mathematics-and-reading-scores-of-fourth--and-eighth-graders-declined-in-most-states-during-pandemic-nations-report-card-shows-301656605.html on August 10, 2024.

Nottingham, J. (2018). *Hattie: Collective efficacy.* Accessed at https://vimeo.com/267382804 on December 4, 2024.

Pfeffer, J., & Sutton, R. I. (2000). *The knowing-doing gap: How smart companies turn knowledge into action.* Boston: Harvard Business School Press.

Robertson, I. H. (2012). *The winner effect: The neuroscience of success and failure.* New York: Thomas Dunne Books.

Robinson, V. M. J., Lloyd, C. A., & Rowe, K. J. (2008). The impact of leadership on student outcomes: An analysis of the differential effects of leadership types. *Educational Administration Quarterly, 44*(5), 635–674.

Schmoker, M. (2004). Learning communities at the crossroads: Toward the best schools we've ever had. *Phi Delta Kappan, 86*(1), 84–88.

Sheely, E. (2014). *The winner effect: How success affects brain chemistry.* Accessed at www.gamification.co/2014/02/21/the-winner-effect/ on June 23, 2024.

Sinek, S. (2011). *Start with why: How great leaders inspire everyone to take action.* London: Penguin Books.

Spiller, K., & Power, K. (2019). *Leading with intention: Eight areas for reflection and planning in your PLC at Work.* Bloomington, IN: Solution Tree Press.

Teague, G. M., & Anfara, V. A., Jr. (2012). Professional learning communities create sustainable change through collaboration. *Middle School Journal, 44*(2), 58–64.

Waters, T., Marzano, R. J., & McNulty, B. (2003). *Balanced leadership: What 30 years of research tells us about the effect of leadership on student achievement* [Working paper]. Denver, CO: McREL.

Wheatley, M., & Frieze, D. (2011, January/February). From hero to host. *Resurgence, 264.* Accessed at www.resurgence.org/magazine/article3282-from-hero-to-host.html on August 11, 2024.

Index

A

agendas, 63, 64

Amabile, T., 12–13

A-Team application, 133, 140.
   See also teams

B

believers, 13

big ideas of a PLC.
   See also PLCs at Work; *specific ideas*
      celebrating commitment to, 3–5
      list of, 2, 5

building leadership, 66–67.
   See also leadership

C

celebrating a focus for learning.
   See focus on learning

celebrating as a catalyst for change
   about, 33–34
   celebrating collective inquiry, 44–47
   celebrating the layers of your PLC, 42–43
   celebrating teammates, 41–42
   competition, ensuring emotionally healthy, 34
   conclusion, 49
   failure and, 47–48
   productive struggle, planning for and celebrating, 34–35, 40
   reproducibles for, 50–53

celebrating collaboration and collective responsibility.
   See collaborative culture and collective responsibility

celebrating for PLC transformation.
   See also PLCs at Work

about, 11–12

conclusion, 29

how should we celebrate, 18–28

reproducibles for, 30–31

why celebrate, 12–18

celebrating results.
  See results orientation

celebrating teammates, 41–42.
  See also teams

celebration dates, 121

celebrations

  collaborative team REAL celebration tool, 84

  connected to learning, 14

  essential standards workshop celebration tool, 87

  planning for celebrations worksheet, 14–15

change, empowering change through results, 112–113, 117–118.
  See also celebrating as a catalyst for change

collaboration

  impact of, 96

  what does it look, sound, and feel like, 97–100

collaborative culture and collective responsibility

  about, 95–96

  celebrating a collaborative culture and collective responsibility, 96–105

  conclusion, 106

  reproducibles for, 107–109

  success criteria, 101–105

collaborative teams.
  See also collaborative culture and collective responsibility; High-Functioning Collaborative Team Award; teams

  celebrating district or school staff, 16

  celebrating the layers of your PLC, 42–43

  celebrating summative results, 132–133, 139–140

  celebrating the right work, 3

collaboration, what does it look, sound, and feel like, 97–100

collaborative team impact checks, 88–91

collaborative team REAL celebration tool, 84

collective inquiry and, 35

collective teacher efficacy and, 40

focus on learning and, 81, 82, 83, 86

guiding coalitions and, 63

results orientation and, 112, 125

team results-oriented commitments and celebrations, 118, 121

what high-functioning collaborative teams look, sound, and feel like, 99

collective inquiry, 44–47

collective responsibility.
  See collaborative culture and collective responsibility

collective teacher efficacy

  about, 95

  collaboration and, 40

  collective inquiry and, 47

  essential standards and, 82

  guiding coalitions and, 62, 68

  impact of, 12, 111

  professional learning and, 16

  results orientation and, 113, 118

commitments

  celebrating commitment to the PLC big ideas, 3–5

  core commitment strands, 4–5

  district and school results-oriented commitments and celebrations, 124–125

  results-oriented commitments, 125

  team results-oriented commitments and celebrations, 118, 121, 124

common formative assessments, 90, 91, 104

common summative assessments, 90, 91, 104

competition, 33, 34, 43

core commitment strands, 4–5

critical questions of a PLC, 20, 80–81, 127. *See also* PLCs at Work

culture shifts

creating a culture shift strategic plan, 24, 28

cultural shifts in a PLC survey tool, 22–23

culture shift strategic plan, 24–27

example Cass High School's PLC culture shift strategic plan, 28

focus, shifts in, 21

current reality, determining your current reality, 21

D

Design in Five (Dimich), 90, 91

Dewey, J., 7

Dimich, N., 90, 91

district staff and personnel

celebrating, 14, 16–18

district and school results-oriented commitments and celebrations, 124–125

Donohoo, J., 95

DuFour, R., 79–80

E

Eaker, R., 21

Eells, R., 95

efficacy. *See* collective teacher efficacy

Erkens, C., 34–35

essential standards

essential standards workshop, 85–88

focus on learning and, 81–82

identifying, 83

learning targets and pacing guides and, 90

REAL process and, 82–83

summative celebrations and, 19

tiers of support and, 127

F

failure, 35, 47–48

feedback, three principles, a horse, and the first day of school—feedback on your leadership, 60–61

film studies, 43

focus, shifts in, 21

focus on learning

about, 79

celebrating a focus on learning and the guaranteed and viable curriculum, 81–91

conclusion, 91

ensuring a guaranteed and viable curriculum, 79–81

reproducibles for, 92–93

formative celebrations, 19, 132

Frieze, D., 61

From Hero to Host (Wheatley and Frieze), 61

fundamentalists, 13

G

guaranteed and viable curriculum

celebrating a focus on learning and, 81–91

ensuring a guaranteed and viable curriculum, 79–81

guiding coalitions

celebrating district of school staff and, 16

creating, 62–64

empowering, 68–69

guiding coalition analysis tool for individual analysis, 72–73

guiding coalition leadership efficacy analysis tool, 70–72

guiding coalitions, celebrating and monitoring the path forward, 73–74

leading with, 60–69

responsibilities of, 67

results focus and, 113

selecting, 64–68

H

Hattie, J., 95, 111

hero leaders, 61

Hersey-Blanchard Situational Leadership Model, 65

High-Functioning Collaborative Team Award. *See also* collaborative teams
- at Bartow County School System, 1–2
- celebrating for PLC transformation, 11
- high-functioning collaborative team application review worksheet, 134–139
- teachers and teams and, 132

I

inquiry failure, 47. *See also* failure

instructional leadership, 62, 66

introduction
- about this book, 5–7
- celebrating commitment to the PLC big ideas, 3–5
- celebrating the right work, 7
- High-Functioning Collaborative Team Award, 1–2
- inspiring innovation, determination, and motivation, 2–3

J

journaling, benefits of, 7

K

Keating, J., 21

Knowing-Doing Gap: How Smart Companies Turn Knowledge Into Action, The (Pfeffer and Sutton), 6

Kolzow, D., 7

Kramer, S., 12–13

L

Leaders of Learning: How District, School, and Classroom Leaders Improve Student Achievement (DuFour and Marzano), 79–80

leadership
- about, 55–56
- conclusion, 74
- guiding coalitions, leading with, 60–69
- guiding coalition leadership, celebrating and monitoring the plan forward, 73–74
- intentional leadership in a PLC, 56–59
- reproducibles for, 75–76
- three principles, a horse, and the first day of school—feedback on your leadership, 59–60

leadership teams, 62, 63, 64, 133

Leading From Within: Building Organizational Leadership Capacity (Kolzow), 7

learning targets
- about, 90
- collaboration and collective responsibility and, 103–104
- essential standards and, 80, 83
- focus on learning and, 81
- teaching-assessing cycle and, 69
- use of, 91

Leverage: Using PLCs to Promote Lasting Improvement in School (Many and Sparks-Many), 104

leveraging celebrations in your leadership. *See* leadership

loose/tight elements, 12, 118, 121, 124

M

Many, T., 104

Marzano, R., 56, 79–80

McNulty, B., 56

Muhammad, A., 13, 105

N

Nation's Report Card, 2

P

pacing guides, 88, 90

Pfeffer, J., 6

planning for celebrations worksheet, 14–15

PLCs at Work. *See also* celebrating for PLC transformation

big ideas of, 2, 3–5

celebrating the layers of, 42–43

critical questions of, 20, 80–81, 127

cultural shifts in a PLC survey tool, 22–23

example Cass High School's PLC culture shift strategic plan, 28

impact of, 44–45

intentional leadership in, 56–59

principals

guiding coalitions and, 63–64, 67–68

intentional leadership and, 57–59

responsibilities of, 61

three principles, a horse, and the first day of school—feedback on your leadership, 59–60

productive struggle

celebrating productive struggle tool, 36–39

planning for and celebrating productive struggle, 34–35, 40

professional learning and professional development

collaborative teams and, 20, 100, 104, 105

guiding coalitions and, 16, 68

results orientation and, 112

Progress Principle, The (Amabile and Kramer), 12–13

progress-monitoring, 113, 121

R

REAL process, 82–83, 84

reproducibles for

chapter 1 journal prompts, 31

chapter 1 reflection questions, 30

chapter 2 journal prompts, 52–53

chapter 2 reflection questions, 50–51

chapter 3 journal prompts, 76

chapter 3 reflection questions, 75

chapter 4 journal prompts, 93

chapter 4 reflection questions, 92

chapter 5 journal prompt, 109

chapter 5 reflection questions, 107–108

chapter 6 journal prompts, 142

chapter 6 reflection questions, 141

response to intervention (RTI), 127

results orientation

about, 111–112, 117

conclusion, 140

district and school results-oriented commitments and celebrations, 124–125

empowering change through results, 112–113, 117–118

reproducibles for, 141–142

"results that matter" worksheet, 114–117

results-oriented success criteria—progress-monitoring and celebration survey, 126

summative results, 132–133, 139

team results-oriented commitments and celebrations, 118, 121, 124

tiers of support, celebrating results through, 127

turning results into celebrations, 118–125

rigor, 88, 91

risk tolerance survey, 48

Robertson, I., 34

Robinson, V., 56

RTI at Work pyramid, 127

S

Schmoker, M., 81

school staff and personnel

celebrating, 14, 16–18

district and school results-oriented commitments and celebrations, 124–125

Sheely, E., 34

"Shift in School Culture, A" (Eaker and Keating), 21

Sinek, S., 6

small wins, creating opportunities for, 19–20

SMART goals

celebrating the layers of your PLC, 42–43

celebrating our team's success the SMART way, 128–131

results orientation and, 117, 125

summative celebrations and, 19

summative results and, 132

tiers of support and, 127

Sparks-Many, S., 104

standards.
See essential standards

static failure, 47.
See also failure

student learning and results-oriented commitments, 125

subcommittees

celebrations and, 18, 19

guiding coalitions and, 67, 68

results orientation and, 113

subcommittee participant table, 68–69

success criteria, collaborative culture and collective responsibility success criteria, 101–105

summative celebrations and results, 19–20, 132–133, 139

superintendents

guiding coalitions and, 60, 61, 62

intentional leadership and, 57, 59

responsibilities of, 61

A-Team application, 133

survivors, 13

surveys

cultural shifts in a PLC survey tool, 22–23

risk tolerance survey, 48

Sutton, R., 6

T

teaching-assessing cycle, 69, 125

teams.
See also collaborative teams

celebrating our team's success the SMART way, 128–131

celebrating teammates, 41–42

A-Team application, 133, 140

team results-oriented commitments and celebrations, 118, 121, 124

tiers of intervention, 127

Transforming School Culture (Muhammad), 13, 105

tweeners, 13

W

Waters, T., 56

Wheatley, M., 61

winner effect, 34

Winner Effect: How Success Affects Brain Chemistry, The (Sheely), 34

Winner Effect: The Neuroscience of Success and Failure, The (Robertson), 34

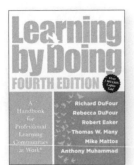

Learning by Doing, Fourth Edition
Richard DuFour, Rebecca DuFour, Robert Eaker, Thomas W. Many, Mike Mattos, and Anthony Muhammad
The fourth edition of this comprehensive action guide provides new strategies for leveraging PLC for a highly effective multitiered system of supports, expert-led guidance on school culture, and a deeper discussion on connecting school improvement to the mission of helping all students succeed.
BKG169

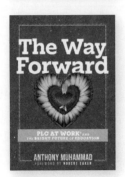

The Way Forward
Anthony Muhammad
Read, reflect, and act with educator and best-selling author Anthony Muhammad as he dives into the educational hurdles of the past, pairing them with tips to face the current challenges in education and ways to build a better tomorrow—all through the PLC at Work® process, a powerful disrupter in the world of education.
BKG159

Beyond PLC Lite
Anthony R. Reibel, Troy Gobble, Mark Onuscheck, and Eric Twadell
Designed for teachers and leaders who want to disrupt the status quo, bust out of PLC Lite, and persistently pursue a culture of continuous improvement, this book carries it all. It emphasizes creating a student-centered approach to teaching and learning in a PLC that prioritizes student agency and efficacy.
BKF913

The 15-Day Challenge
Maria Nielsen
Simplicity of the PLC process and energy to drive the work are essential for teams to collaborate successfully. Author Maria Nielsen provides you with the structure and tools you need to confidently utilize both of these staples to become a high-functioning professional learning community.
BKF969

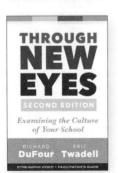

Through New Eyes, Second Edition
Richard DuFour and Eric Twadell
Discover what a collaborative culture of student-centered learning looks like through the eyes of a struggling learner. Recorded at the award-winning Adlai E. Stevenson High School in Lincolnshire, Illinois, this video workshop is a great way to build unity around the why behind PLC at Work®: learning for all.
DIG119

Solution Tree | Press

Visit SolutionTree.com or call 800.733.6786 to order.

Quality team learning **from authors you trust**

Global PD Teams is the first-ever **online professional development resource designed to support your entire faculty on your learning journey.** This convenient tool offers daily access to videos, mini-courses, eBooks, articles, and more packed with insights and research-backed strategies you can use immediately.

GET STARTED
SolutionTree.com/**GlobalPDTeams**
800.733.6786